The Fearless School Leader

Making the Right Decisions

Cynthia McCabe

Eye On Education
6 Depot Way West, Suite 106
Larchmont, NY 10538
(914) 833-0551
(914) 833-0761 fax
www.eyeoneducation.com

Library of Congress Cataloging-in-Publication Data

McCabe, Cynthia.
The fearless school leader : making the right decisions/by Cynthia McCabe.
    p.   cm.
Includes bibliographical references.
ISBN 978-1-59667-188-1
1. School management and organization.
2. Educational leadership.
3. Decision making.
I. Title.
LB2805.M33215 2011
371.2—dc23   2011014642

10 9 8 7 6 5 4 3 2 1

Sponsoring Editor: Robert Sickles
Production Editor: Lauren Beebe
Copyeditor: Lauren Beebe
Designer and Compositor: Matthew Williams
Cover Designer: Dave Strauss

Also Available from EYE ON EDUCATION

The Principal as Student Advocate:
A Guide for Doing What's Best for All Students
M. Scott Norton, Larry K. Kelly, & Anna Battle

Communicate and Motivate:
The School Leader's Guide to Effective Communication
Shelly Arneson

Rigor in Your School:
A Toolkit for Leaders
Ronald Williamson & Barbara R. Blackburn

Schools Where Teachers Lead:
What Successful Leaders Do
John S. Bell, Tony Thacker, & Franklin P. Schargel

Problem-Solving Tools and Tips for School Leaders
Cathie E. West

Principals Who Dare to Care
A. William Place

The Principalship from A to Z
Ronald Williamson & Barbara R. Blackburn

162 Keys to School Success:
Be the Best, Hire the Best, Train, Inspire, and Retain the Best
Franklin P. Schargel

Differentiation Is an Expectation:
A School Leader's Guide to Building a Culture of Differentiation
Kimberly Kappler Hewitt & Daniel K. Weckstein

Rigorous Schools and Classrooms: Leading the Way
Ronald Williamson & Barbara R. Blackburn

Leading School Change: 9 Strategies to Bring Everybody on Board
Todd Whitaker

Executive Skills for Busy School Leaders
Christopher Hitch & David C. Coley

To my husband, Jim, for his insights and encouragement

Acknowledgements

Thank you to the following educators for their professional conversation and for lending knowledge and expertise to this work:

- Cynthia Dillon
- Donn Hicks
- Thomas Hill
- Steven Johnson
- Stacey Kopnitsky
- William Piercy
- Thomasina Piercy
- Patricia Reed
- Thomas Saunders
- Nicholas Shockney
- John Seaman
- Nancy Short
- Andrea Townsend
- Genee Varlack
- Steve Warner

Table of Contents

About the Author

Cynthia McCabe is the Director of Elementary Schools for Carroll County Public Schools in Westminster, Maryland. Over her career in the state of Maryland, she has been a classroom teacher, a gifted and talented resource specialist, an assistant principal, a principal, and an elementary supervisor of curriculum and instruction. Cindy has also worked as an adjunct instructor at Towson University in Towson, Maryland, supervising administrative interns and teaching courses in the educational leadership division. She has a passion for improving the effectiveness of public schools, enabling students to successfully pursue their professional callings. Cindy can be reached by email at cindy@mccabe.us.com.

Free Downloads

Some of the figures discussed and displayed in this book are also available on Eye On Education's website as Adobe Acrobat files. Permission has been granted to purchasers of this book to download these figures and print them.

You can access these free downloads by visiting Eye On Education's website: **www.eyeoneducation.com**. From the home page, click on FREE, then click on Supplemental Downloads. Alternatively, you can search or browse our website to find this book, then click on "Log in to Access Supplemental Downloads."

Your book-buyer access code is **FSL-7188-1**.

Index of Free Downloads

Introduction

It took me twelve years to do it. I was married in 1992, moved four times, renovated an entire house, and finally got up the nerve. To do what, you ask?

Skydive?

No.

Bungie jump?

Nope.

It took me twelve years to muster the nerve to bake a turkey—a whole turkey. I know it sounds silly. But the process really frightened me. I knew there were unsavory parts hiding out inside the cavity that needed to be removed before baking. How would I identify these mystery parts and what if I missed one and left it inside, thinking it was an ingrown wing or an extension of the neck? Then there was the tying up of the bird using some kind of string and an intricate lacing technique—pretty intimidating when Martha Stewart demonstrated it. Most importantly, how would I know when it was done? There were mathematical equations to utilize involving the weight of the bird and minutes per pound. And when piercing the thigh, the novice cook was warned to avoid touching bone, as this might give a false temperature reading. How would I know if the tip of the thermometer was touching a bone? I could just imagine the scorn of my dinner guests as they bit into their thigh meat to find it still raw inside.

Okay. I can hear you saying, "Come on, Cindy. Just bake the darn turkey and move on!" But that's just the point. While this fear may sound ridiculous to many, it wasn't to me. Though not mortal fear, these feelings were very real—real enough to keep me from ever hosting Thanksgiving dinner. I was afraid enough of being judged to avoid action.

Flash back with me now to 1975, to a day I'll never erase from my memory. I was three years old, watching *The Price Is Right* with my mother and twelve-year-old sister, who was sick and home from school.

"I think I smell smoke," my sister whispered.

This was all it took to eject my mother from her chair. She ran up the stairs and threw open the door to the first floor. "Fire!" we heard her scream out, as smoke billowed down the stairwell and began filling the room. Running upstairs in total panic, my sister left me—alone.

The scene is burned into my brain like a movie in slow motion. The force of the fire roared into the room like a freight train, overtaking all other sound. It was too late for me to try to climb the steep staircase, which I could only scale by crawling up each step, one at a time. Within seconds, the room went black; I closed my eyes to keep out the burning smoke. Every breath scorched my throat and lungs. With my arms out in front of me, I felt my way to the television cart in the corner and crawled behind it, curling into a ball. At three years old, I was struck with the realization that I could die. Everything went numb.

This is certainly an example of mortal fear—fear that is strong enough to paralyze the mind. What I didn't state in my retelling is that there was an outside door downstairs in my house. You could get to it by walking through the clubroom, opening a door and walking through to the laundry room. So why didn't I try to escape using the door? All I can tell you is that when my senses were engulfed by fire, my logical brain shut off.

This is the nature of fear. It backs us into a corner like a bully and makes us accept defeat. Whether it's mortal fear (fear of physical harm) or emotional fear (fear of harm to the ego), this powerful feeling keeps us from taking the very actions that could improve our lives—or even save them.

In our personal lives, fear can wreak havoc on relationships with family and friends. It can keep us static, unwilling to try new things or participate in social opportunities and activities we enjoy.

In our professional lives, fear causes us to act in ways that are out of alignment with the worthy goals of public education. It diverts our attention and shifts our energy to areas that, in the long run, do not help students or teachers.

What has fear kept you from doing lately? What decisions have you made out of fear? For yourself? For your teachers? For your students?

Drawing from the fields of neuroscience, psychology, organizational development, and educational leadership, this book acknowledges the role that fear plays in schools across the country, analyzes why it is so powerful, and provides the steps to overcome it. In the following chapters, school leaders are shown how to make the fearless decisions to improve their schools. Throughout the text, Opportunities for Reflection are included to support positive change in thoughts, feelings, and professional action.

1

The Power of Fear

After spending years in the field of education, I've come to the conclusion that there are two major causes of failing schools:

1. school leaders who aren't sure what to do in order to improve student achievement, and
2. school leaders who *know* what they *should* do, yet don't to do it.

This is not to say there aren't other reasons for poor achievement. Low parent involvement, inequities in school funding, and high student mobility rates are just a few of the challenges that must be acknowledged. But the purpose here is to explore a larger issue that looms over the rest, one that has been given little attention within the field of education—and one that is within our control as leaders.

For over a decade, experts such as Michael Fullan, Doug Reeves, and Mike Schmoker have been very clear about what school leaders need to do in order to increase student achievement. But very little has changed in school improvement practices across the country as a result. In my experience (and I'm betting all across this country), stressed out and exhausted principals wrestle daily to make decisions and take actions that are in alignment with what they know is best for students.

For far too long, the educational community has ignored the elephant in the room—fear. Why? Well, it's just not easy conversation. In fact, it can be downright uncomfortable to talk about. But until we're willing to explore the emotional side of decision making and its impact on school improvement, the status quo will remain intact, and students will suffer. The intention of this book is to begin a much-needed dialogue about the power of fear, first internally with the reader and then within the professional community. Only then will there be a chance to increase understandings that have the power to change current school practices.

The scope of this book is broad, encompassing topics such as data-driven decision making, teacher evaluation, and increasing accountability—each of which could most certainly make up an entire book. This range, however, is purposeful and necessary, as the power of fear is palpable in every aspect of school leadership. It is my hope that this information will increase your daily awareness of the potential effects of fear on your decision making, and arm you with the vital understandings to rise above it to make fearless decisions for yourself and for students.

Eyes Wide Open

Let's be honest—there aren't always external rewards awaiting those who make tough decisions. In fact, some systems unknowingly reward leaders who placate stakeholders at the expense of taking actions to improve student achievement. These are the leaders who may be beloved by their faculties and communities, but who are unable to substantially impact student learning. In many districts, the principal who begins to make difficult yet necessary changes is met with disapproval from teachers, students, parents, and superiors. We've all heard of the principal who is let go after too many stakeholders make formal complaints against him. This reality sets up an internal struggle that each school leader must face. Will I choose to be liked or to put student achievement first? Safety or risk? While the two paths aren't mutually exclusive, and in fact, will cross and intertwine over the course of a day, month, year, and career, one must choose which will provide the foundational value for action.

Until one is hoisted into the high-pressure role of school administrator, there is no way to comprehend the complexities and competing interests that assert themselves into the myriad of decisions made within the course of a day. It's easy for an observer to judge a school leader for decisions that seem to be made for the purposes of efficiency and peace in the faculty lounge. I know I did my share of judging while in the classroom. However, that ended when my first administration position began. By the end of my first week of crying kindergartners, complaining parents, voluminous paperwork, restrictive policies, tight budgets, and stressed out teachers, I completely empathized with all of my previous administrators and the decisions they had made. My eyes were opened to the realities of the role.

Still, deep down, I wanted to be different, to swim against the current mercilessly dragging me down, weakening my will. And I think school leaders across the country feel the same way.

New Understandings About the Brain

The field of neuroscience is exploding with new discoveries, many of which have great implications for varied professions. Fields of study such as psychology, sales and marketing, criminal justice, politics, and business management have already begun capitalizing on this new knowledge. While the field of education has shown interest in brain science as it relates to student learning, it has not yet capitalized on the way it can impact school leadership practices. These understandings have the power to change the way we approach school reform.

Let's begin with the brain. We all have not one brain, but three. Neuroscientists have identified them as the old brain (otherwise known as the reptilian brain), the middle brain, and the new brain.

◆ The new brain thinks. It processes rational data.
◆ The middle brain feels. It processes emotions and gut feelings.
◆ The old brain decides. It takes into account the input from the other two brains, but the old brain is the actual trigger of decision. (Renvoise & Morin, 2007, p. 6)

According to neuroscientist Robert Ornstein, the old brain, located at the top of the spine, was the first to develop and is concerned with our survival. (Orstein & Thompson, 1991, p. 24) It makes sense that our fight-or-flight response is generated from here. And although the old brain "listens to" input from both our middle brain and our new brain, there is increasing evidence that the middle brain has more sway, causing our emotions to influence decisions more than rational thought. Information processed in the new brain, or cortex, is considered only through the emotional filter of the middle brain when a decision is made by the old brain. In *Emotionomics*, Dan Hill (2008) stated that the middle brain's "key activity is to assign gut-level value to the situations we encounter" (p. 17). Dr. Joseph LeDoux, a leading neuroscientist, said in *Emotional Brain* that the amygdale, which is found in the middle brain, "has a greater influence on the cortex [the new brain] than the cortex has on the amygdale, allowing emotional arousal to dominate and control thinking" (Renvoise & Morin, 2007, p. 8). Like Antonio Damasio stated in *Descartes' Error*, "We are not thinking machines that feel, we are feeling machines that think" (p. 16).

Marketing experts have understood this for quite some time, which is why advertising campaigns appeal to our emotions. A great example of this is the current campaign for Dove soap. Do their advertisements focus on how much cleaner you'll be if you use Dove soap? Or how much cheaper Dove soap is in comparison to Ivory? No. Instead, their commercials and print ads focus on helping women (and now men) *feel* good about themselves. Their messages promote positive body image, which supports positive self-image. And everyone wants to buy a product that will make them feel safe and accepted, right? "Yes, at times people will analyze the 'facts' vigorously," writes Hill (2008), "But emotions are basic and more dominant. Remember: we feel before we think, and those reactions are subconscious, immediate and inescapable" (p. 24).

The Nature of Fear

Of all the emotions that influence us on a daily basis, negative emotions are the most powerful because "survival instincts dictate being more alert to hearing bad news than good news" (Hill, 2008, p. 49). Our old brain is always on the lookout for anything that might threaten us, either physically or psychologically. Logically then, "fear is the single most important emotion. . . . In fear's basic script, we seek to escape some perceived danger in order to protect ourselves" (p. 51). In essence, when we feel fear, the mind is trying to alert us to impending pain—either physical or psychological, so we may change direction and avoid it or defend ourselves from it. This reaction is also known as the fight-or-flight response. When the situation is indeed dangerous, this old brain decision to battle or flee helps to ensure our survival. However, in many situations, this response is counterproductive. Psychologist and consultant Ken Hultman (1998) states that, "People often escape situations they should face, avoid opportunities that could help them learn, and attack people with whom they should be building alliances. . . . [the fight-or-flight response] does nothing to help us make something positive happen in our lives" (p. 16).

Fear is the elephant in the room. Fear grips us and disables us from making decisions that will move our schools forward. We must acknowledge its power and make it a part of our professional consideration and dialogue. How many of your decisions have been driven by fear?

At one point, a friend of mine in business management became so frightened of some of the controversial decisions confronting her at work, that she began calling in sick. She used this strategy to avoid heated meetings and appointments that she couldn't face. Needless to say, the state of her department did not improve and problems that could have been solved early, ended up snowballing into much bigger issues.

Dan Hill's (2008) review of the research shows us that fear causes cautious decision making where we are wary of the outcome. And at its worst, fear can make us freeze entirely, leaving us paralyzed (p. 29). This was certainly the case in my three-year-old brain as the smoke engulfed my body, keeping me from processing the available escape route through the basement door to the outside.

Fear not only has the ability to keep us frozen mentally, it can also stop us from making decisions in a timely fashion. This can be observed in the School Improvement Team that discusses the possibilities of what might be done for students, but never executes a plan. That would mean taking a risk. And what if they made the wrong decision or upset staff members in the process? It's much safer to talk, just as it had been safer for me to think about roasting the turkey.

Am I Worthy?

Humans spend their lives in pursuit of meeting needs. First come the physical needs of food, water, and shelter. We work hard when we're young—going to college, choosing a career, and procuring a job—to ensure that we can meet these needs. And hopefully along the way, we select a path that can meet our emotional needs as well, for these are what serve to offer us fulfillment. Ken Hultman (1998) identifies our greatest need as having worth or value as a person, both in our own eyes and the eyes of others:

> Everything we do reflects on our worth in one way or another. We are always motivated to validate our worth, but since we can never be sure what's going to happen next, we're also vulnerable to having our sense of worth weakened. Therefore, although the need to feel worthy can propel us forward, fear of unworthiness can hold us back. (p. 17)

One hot and sunny day last summer, I relaxed with close friends and family, bobbing on the waves of the Chesapeake Bay. During lunch, one of my childhood friends announced that she was actively planning to leave her job at a top-ranked university, a job that has provided well for her and her family. She explained that she was beginning to feel a sense of emptiness in her current work and longed to pursue something of worth. Unsure of exactly which direction to take, she said, "I just want to do something that will make a difference in the world. I want all my hard work to be worthwhile."

I don't think this sentiment is unique to her. I know I have felt that way at different points in my career. Many go into helping professions such as teaching, nursing, counseling, etc. due to a drive for doing something impactful—something that will help others and the greater good. But for some who enter these fields with that desire—and the energy and idealism to match—burnout awaits after they work themselves to the point of exhaustion in pursuit of finding worth. Are you feeling this way as a school leader? How many of your teachers are in this situation right now?

This search for significance is supported by four subneeds that help us to feel worthy. And just as our need for self-worth is partnered with the fear of being unworthy, our subneeds are partnered with corresponding fears:

- ◆ Need for Mastery vs. Fear of Failure
- ◆ Need for Respect vs. Fear of Judgment
- ◆ Need for a Sense of Meaning and Purpose vs. Fear of Purposelessness
- ◆ Need for Acceptance vs. Fear of Rejection (Hultman, 1998, p. 18)

The drive for a sense of worth compels one to try to be perceived as both a competent person and a good person. Every day in our schools, these personal and social needs play themselves out in the lives of school leaders and teachers. Each need and its corresponding fear drive us to make decisions and take certain actions or prevent us from taking them. This dual nature can make our striving to fulfill needs a double-edged sword. Let's take a closer look at each need.

Need for Mastery vs. Fear of Failure

I've had the same recurring nightmare now for 20 years. I am in college. It is the week before finals and I haven't attended any of my classes in weeks. I haven't completed the assignments. I don't even know what assignments have been assigned! I don't remember which buildings my classes are in or who is teaching them.

I look around and quickly spot someone who I recognize from one of my classes. But when I ask him to fill me in on what I've missed, he smirks and says, "Where have you been? It's too late to get caught up now. You're going to fail." With that statement, a sense of doom overwhelms me and I wake up in a painful, sweaty panic.

Why do I keep having the dream? This is probably a question for a good therapist, but I think I know myself well enough to understand the reason. I have always been tormented by the fear of failure—afraid of not working hard enough to pass whatever life test was at hand.

And that is the nature of the fear of failure. According to Gallup International Research & Education Center leaders Marcus Buckingham and Donald Clifton (2001), it stays hidden when we can blame our shortcomings on others

Opportunity for Reflection

What decisions for your school have you made out of fear?

What actions have you avoided out of fear?

What career accomplishments have given you a sense of mastery?

What past failures have kept you from trying new things professionally?

or on particular circumstances, but strikes when we've tried to accomplish something on our own, drawing on what we consider to be our talents—especially when others are watching: "The most persistent and damaging are those times when we pick out one of our strengths, stake a claim, go all out, and yet still fail." These kinds of painful experiences during childhood and adolescence can convince us to play it safe and only try for accomplishments that are easily within reach.

On the flip side, the need for mastery goads us to take the risk and accomplish great things. It saves us from a life of mediocrity, one in which we squander our innate gifts. We're all familiar with Maslow's hierarchy of needs. According to Maslow, this need to master and accomplish exists in the growth or esteem needs section of his hierarchy, above the needs for physical well-being/security and belonging. It is a higher-level need that many pursue only after lower needs have been met (Cherry, 2011).

The real trick is in the ability to overcome self-protection instincts in order to continually grow and develop. Otherwise, we stay stuck in our current place. How has the fear of failure affected you?

Need for Respect vs. Fear of Judgment

Every time I tune into the television show *Cops*, someone is explaining to authorities that they became violent because they were disrespected. This explanation is given over and over again by everyone from gang members to domestic abusers. And in the east Baltimore neighborhood in which I grew up, the regular consequence for disrespect was an immediate fight. Being disrespected cuts to the quick of self-worth and strips us of our dignity. And for some, the emotional pain is too great to bear. They will do whatever it takes to keep it from happening again.

Conversely, garnering "respect signals a full recognition as a person" (De Cremer & Mulder, 2007, p. 440). It communicates that our moral worth is equal to others in society and that we are thus deserving of the same dignity as anybody else (p. 440). Feeling respected by others also meets our need to have a good reputation within the community, which leads to positive self-identity (p. 442).

This need for respect can drive us to act in an ethical manner and to make constructive decisions. In the field of education, that should mean doing what's best for students. But this can be a risky proposition, one in which gaining respect might elude us.

Last month in Central Falls, Rhode Island, the School Board of Trustees voted 5–2 to fire every teacher at the school. U.S. Secretary of Education Arne Duncan stated that he "applauded" them for "showing courage and doing the right thing for kids" (Jordan, 2010). One of the board trustees, B.K. Nordan, a graduate of Central Falls High School and a teacher in Providence made his opinion clear, asserting that the situation wasn't about worker's rights, but about student's rights; and that no statistics showed that teachers were being effective enough with students.

> The rhetoric that these are poor students . . . is exactly why we need you to step up. . . . This city needs it more than anybody. I demand of you that you demand more of yourself and those around you. (Jordan, 2010)

Nordan laid down an expectation of increased respect for students, for the job, and for themselves as professionals. While I can't say whether or not the board's decision was right, it is safe to say that it was risky. I agree with Arne Duncan that firing everyone in the school certainly took courage—courage in the face of judgment. And judgment is just what the board got. Teachers in attendance at the meeting cried and shouted at them. Students gathered there to support the school's staff. George Nee, president of the Rhode Island chapter of the American Federation of Labor and Congress of Industrial Organizations (AFL-CIO), called the decision "immoral, illegal, unjust, irresponsible, disgraceful, and disrespectful" (Jordan, 2010).

The flip side of the need for respect is the fear of judgment. And unfortunately, fear of judgment has the power to keep us from taking needed moral action. How many of us could have made this tough decision, knowing the derision we would face? Often times when a school leader makes a decision that is in the best interest of students, a stakeholder group is angered or agitated. And when that anger is expressed as judgment, it hurts. We all wish to be viewed as good people, worthy of respect. But since "good" is subjective, the definition and embodiment is bound to change in the eye of each beholder, leaving us all vulnerable to negative judgment. It is our reaction to

> ## *Opportunity for Reflection*
>
> What actions have you taken out of personal conviction that have also earned respect from your teachers?
>
> What actions have you taken out of personal conviction that have drawn judgment from teachers or parents?
>
> What decisions have you made out of fear of judgment? How did these decisions impact students?

this fact that determines future success. If we allow the fear of judgment to handcuff our decision making, then we are sentenced to a professional life of walking on eggshells, being ruled by our old and middle brains. Students deserve leaders with more courage than this.

Need for a Sense of Meaning and Purpose vs. Fear of Purposelessness

Each year, countless college graduates walk across the stage and receive the degrees that will help qualify them to teach. Their faces glow with the promise and possibility of changing the world, one student at a time—long before the financial, emotional, and relational implications of teaching have had a chance to introduce themselves. In this psychological sweet spot, there is deep satisfaction caused by a strong sense of meaning and purpose. And if their personal mission of making a difference aligns with that of the school into which they are hired, teachers, students, and the organization as a whole will benefit.

At their core, people want to work to give their lives direction. This should be easy in the field of education. It might be difficult for workers to find meaning and purpose when they are in jobs that don't offer pathways to develop and express professional skills, knowledge, and creativity, as well as a moral imperative to succeed. But educators aren't working the line in a factory to assemble widgets. No, educators have one of the most important jobs in the world—one that must be done expertly in order to ensure the future good of society.

Yet, over time, many dedicated educators (both teachers and administrators) can begin to develop a sense of purposelessness. I observed this as an administrator when teachers began to question the value of spending so

Opportunity for Reflection

Why did you decide to be a school leader?
Do you still feel a sense of purpose in your role as a school leader?
  If not, what circumstances have led to this feeling?

many hours planning, instructing, and assessing without seeing significant changes in student achievement. What is the purpose of trying? I could see them becoming deeply discouraged. Worried, I began to question what could I do to inspire and restore a commitment to our mission.

We are wise to fear purposelessness. Because when it sets in, our sense of worth decreases and our moral compass is compromised, causing us to lose hope and accept futility. It's easy for purposelessness to sneak in, replacing the zeal to do important work. We see it in the congressman who enters Washington D.C., energized and ready to do the work of the people, only to find himself bogged down in "politics," seeking self-preservation over all else. There's the attorney who starts her career with the passion to help people get justice and ends up disillusioned with the "cracks" in the system, choosing to focus only on making herself wealthier. Then there's the social worker who dedicates himself to protecting children, yet finds himself under the burden of an unrealistic case load and an unsupportive judicial system.

We must be on the watch for purposelessness, alert to its beginnings. For if it overtakes school leaders, there is little hope for teachers and students. Fighting it begins with this truth: school leaders have one of the most important jobs in the world. Every single day, we impact the lives of hundreds of children—their ability to pursue their chosen careers, their ability to compete in a global marketplace, their ability to pursue their own happiness. We impact the future of our country by turning out students who are both competent and creative enough to solve the enormous challenges facing our society. To fall down on the job isn't an option. We either need to get out or commit fully once and for all.

Need for Acceptance vs. Fear of Rejection

Ah, peer pressure. We've all experienced it—this human need for being accepted by our tribes, including family, friends, and coworkers. Besides survival concerns, it's one of our most basic needs, even coming before our esteem needs, according to Maslow (Cherry, 2011). In their popular work *Social and Human Nature*, Roy Baumeister and Brad Bushman (2008) state, "The need to belong is called a need, rather than merely a want, because when it is thwarted people suffer more than just being unhappy. . . . Failure to satisfy the need to belong leads to significant health problems" (p. 331). And that's what makes this need especially problematic.

One administrator saw this first hand when she and her faculty devised a new approach to help all students master basic literacy skills. The selected intervention would have a deep impact on the everyday instruction happening in classrooms. Within a very short time, the results of their efforts were very positive. The impact of the new intervention was undeniable and student achievement data began to reflect it.

Curious, some colleagues from around the state started to call and ask her what she was doing differently. She and her staff were happy to share what they had learned with anyone showing interest. But the reaction from one particular principal would stay with her for a long time. Upon hearing about the instructional strategies utilized in the intervention program, she responded, "I like it a lot and I'd like to use it. But I don't think I can. None of my friends would speak to me."

This principal was aware of the fact that conformity plays a major part in gaining and sustaining belonging within a group. People are naturally attracted to and feel most comfortable with those similar to themselves (Baumeister & Bushman, 2008, p. 332). The need for acceptance and fear of rejection outweighed this principal's need for respect and sense of purpose. She felt she needed to show that her beliefs and values were congruent with those of her professional group, or face exclusion. So instead of being able

Opportunity for Reflection

Reflect upon a time when you felt rejected by colleagues, teachers, or parents. What caused the reaction? Did you do what you felt was best for students?

Reflect upon a time when you took a specific action in order to gain acceptance from colleagues, teachers, or parents. What was the decision/action? What was the impact on students?

What are some healthy ways to meet the need for acceptance? What are the personal implications of putting students' needs and your school's needs before your own emotional needs?

to focus on increasing student performance, her mind was on the uneasiness she would feel if she went forward with the intervention. This kind of atmosphere inhibits creativity and workers' contributions to the organization (Hultman, 1998, p. 39).

While the need for acceptance is valid, it can be one of the most dangerous needs we strive to fulfill in the workplace. That is why it is imperative to surround ourselves with colleagues who share a dedication to achieving results above all else and a commitment to the acceptance of diverse ideas within our schools.

So, in the end, fear has more control over our professional lives than most of us realize or would feel comfortable admitting. And unfortunately, there is no quick solution to this very human predicament. But although it isn't as easy as swallowing a pill, there are antidotes to making fear-based decisions that allow us to become the courageous leaders we all aspire to be.

2

The Antidote: Fearless Decisions

Suppose you were taking a relaxing stroll down the beach on a hot summer day when the sight of a small child struggling to stay afloat in the breakers stopped you in your tracks. Quickly scanning the area, you saw no lifeguard or anyone else capable of helping. In this situation, who wouldn't run into the ocean and swim out to help the drowning victim? Without even thinking, most people would take swift action to ensure the survival of the child.

Lower vs. Higher Concerns

In Chapter 1, we explored the natural tendency of the brain toward using emotional versus rational input when making decisions. Fear was examined in detail, as it has the power to engage the old, reptilian brain faster than any other emotion. Then the four fears that tend to rule our professional decisions were uncovered, along with the needs that motivate action. They all center around the desire for self-worth, and while that is the pinnacle of our needs, self-worth is a need which is very personal in nature. Therefore, I character-ize our emotional needs, along with physical needs, as lower concerns, things that are important to us because they directly affect us. The reason for this description lies not in the concern's level of importance, but on the *focus* of the concern. When we focus on issues like our ability to feed ourselves, our abil-ity to acquire friends, or our degree of professional competence, the center of attention is the self. In contrast, I characterize concerns that have an outward focus as higher concerns. When we hold higher concerns, we put someone else's well-being above our own. This would include a focus on what's best for a particular student, for a school, for public education, or for society at large.

Let's take the beach example above. When you make the split-second decision to swim into the ocean to save the child, your concern is higher in nature, since you've prioritized the safety of another human being over personal concerns. However, if you were to stand on the beach and watch the child struggle, all the while worrying about your own safety if you tried to help, or the scrutiny of sunbathers critiquing your breaststroke, your concern would be lower in nature. It would revolve around protecting or feeding your ego rather than on helping another in need. I realize that this is an extreme example. But, often times as school leaders, we do spend much of our time dealing with the lower concerns of teachers, parents, and ourselves while higher, vital concerns are all but ignored. During the course of the day, we hear from:

◆ The parent who wants her child's report card grade changed in order to feel good sharing it with friends and neighbors (need for respect/fear of judgment).
◆ The teacher who complains that her instructional practices are being criticized by a parent (need for mastery/fear of failure).
◆ The parent who requests his son's math class be changed so the child may be instructed with students that he has determined to be suitable friends (need for social acceptance/fear of rejection).

I'm sure if we took note of how our time is used, we'd discover that helping people (including ourselves) resolve lower-level concerns monopolizes a majority of it.

A Commitment to Higher Concerns

So, how do we overcome the natural wiring of the brain in order to more fully utilize the new brain, and fearlessly work for the common good? To start, we need to get back in touch with why we entered this occupation. I trust it wasn't for the money or the prestige. In most cases, teaching and leading felt right and felt natural. It was a part of who we wanted to become, in order to fulfill what I believe to be a calling. We can't back out of that now. We just need to learn how to control the fear that is our biggest obstacle to following the soul's chosen path.

The first step towards making fearless decisions as a leader is to develop an awareness of the thoughts and emotions you experience around self-preservation. You can then begin to monitor these, and when ego needs arise, make a conscious commitment to higher concerns. This doesn't mean that you won't have to deal with the lower concerns of the stakeholders around you. In fact, it is important to understand the root ego needs of those concerns and work to acknowledge and address them. What it does mean is that you will be cognizant of your own motivations, and when you find them to be lower, make the choice to move to a higher place. In doing so, you will change the focus from personal concerns to greater issues that impact the welfare of others, namely students. I promise that in putting off the chase for personal pursuits in order to focus upon helping students achieve, in the end, you will obtain the truest sense of self-worth you've ever experienced. According to Paul Houston and Stephen Sokolow (2006), "Our sense of purpose and our sense of meaning grow when our underlying motivation is to help others" (p. 2).

If, after reading this chapter, you have determined that your true intention is to climb the bureaucratic ladder of education to gain financial security or power, then I beg you to put this book down and get out of the field of education as quickly as possible. It is the moral decision. There simply is no room here for professionals who cannot keep personal concerns in check enough to take the risks necessary for transforming public schooling in the United States.

Reality Check: Higher Concerns

Public school education is in a precarious position, and therefore, so are all of the students within this country's system. The following achievement statistics from the U.S. Department of Education Institute of Educational Sciences tell the story:

◆ Long-term trends in science and mathematics show declines in student achievement in the 1970s and early 1980s, followed by modest increases. For example, the mathematics score averages of 17-year-olds declined from 1973 to 1982, then increased to a level in 1996 similar to the 1973 level.

◆ Long term trends in reading achievement show minimal changes across the assessment years.

◆ Data from the Third International Mathematics and Science Study (TIMSS) suggests that the relative international standing of U.S. students declines as they progress through school. In both subject areas, our students perform above the international average in grade 4, close to the international average in grade 8, and considerably below it in grade 12.

◆ In twelfth grade, the achievement scores of both our overall student population tested on general mathematics and science knowledge, and of our more advance students tested in mathematics and physics, were well below the international average. (National Center for Education Statistics, 2010)

A recent issue of *Newsweek* magazine included a scathing review of the effectiveness of the public school system, lamenting the shameful deterioration of American students' ranking against Europeans from first to approximately tenth, based on standardized testing (Thomas & Wingert, 2010).

With this reality, how will our students be able to compete for jobs in the global marketplace? And how might this impact America's economic standing in the world, as well as the standard of living for its citizens? People across the country are becoming more aware of this dire situation, and are therefore beginning to demand a new competency from their public schools. Some seem to have come to the end of their tolerance for a system that cannot show progress. In an article entitled, "Do Away with Public Schools," in the *Los Angeles Times*, Jonah Goldberg didn't hold back. He chided public schools for their charming tag lines and sentiments, all the while hurting the students they say they care about. He goes on to state that a sure-fire way to leave students behind is to put them in government schools.

Americans want universal education, just as they want universally safe food. But nobody believes that the government should run 90% of the restaurants, farms and supermarkets. Why should it run 90% of the schools—particularly when it gets terrible results? (Goldberg, 2007)

Similarly, the *Washington Post* ran an article entitled, "Traditional Schools Aren't Working. Let's Move Learning Online." There, the author states, "National surveys find that parents despair over the quality of education in the United States—and they're right to, as test results confirm again and again . . . it's time to take online education seriously—because we've tried everything else" (Mangu-Ward, 2010).

This is just a sample of the frustration and outrage that exists today. Everyone involved in public education should take seriously the imperatives of its critics, including the expansion of vouchers, charter schools, home schools, and privatization. This higher concern should firstly acknowledge the problem—the unintentional malpractice that is currently perpetrated on students in many public schools across the country each day. Instead of defending ourselves and making excuses for the failures of public education, we must acknowledge where we've come short and recommit to doing whatever it takes to get better results. If not, then our students' inability to procure jobs, along with the United States' sliding standard of living would be, in large part, our fault. Our school leaders must know what the stakes are. Karin Chenoweth (2008) describes the stakes in her research on academic success in unexpected schools:

> [I]f their students don't get a good education, they face the probability of a lifetime of poverty and dependence. "We have got to expand [our students'] horizons or we are still signing their death warrants," principal coach Martha Barber tells principals she works with in Alabama. (p. 217)

Secondly, educators must wake up and realize that if we are unable to turn things around, we may see the end of public schooling. Most educators believe that when they sign a teaching contract, they are guaranteed a job for life. Receiving tenure only strengthens this belief. And principals work under the assumption that unless they cause an uproar in the school community, their jobs are equally safe. The truth is, in the current climate, none of our jobs are safe. Reconstitution is already occurring in many schools across the nation and is even sometimes a requirement if districts are to receive certain funding. Moreover, Race to the Top funding requires districts to tie school performance with principal evaluations and student performance with teacher evaluation. So, even if the public wasn't fed up with the failures of the public school system and wasn't actively seeking alternatives to it, educators would still have reason to take pause. It isn't safe to keep doing what we've always done. Helen Keller once said, "Security is mostly a superstition. It does not exist in nature, nor do the children of men as a whole experience it. . . . Life is either a daring adventure or nothing" (Kushner, 2009, p. 112).

Yet if public education were to disappear, higher concerns than shifting employment opportunities for educators would dominate the national dialogue. It would mean the death of democratic education as an ideal. The impact of complete privatization, or denying a free and appropriate education to every child in the country, could have an even more devastating impact on national achievement than do the failures of our current system.

Redemption

Redeeming public education will require both direction and permission at the federal and state levels of government, which has already begun around the country with the inception of the common core standards; replacing tenure tracks with value-added options; and providing opportunities for merit pay. But, like most other successful movements, the improvement of public schooling will have to be a grassroots movement that begins with leaders like you and me. Will you embody Helen Keller's sentiment and join this daring adventure?

Set Your New Intention

In the late 1990's, Martin Seligman, a psychologist at the University of Pennsylvania, founded the positive psychology movement, a new area of study devoted to discovering what makes individuals and groups thrive (Seligman & Sikszentmihalyi, 2000, p. 6). This movement has shown that we *can* overcome our brain wiring as well as negative emotions and habits in order to flourish. Many doctors, scholars, and popular figures have contributed to this body of knowledge; long before Seligman, men like Henry Maslow and William James were already writing and researching the subject (Gable & Haidt, 2005, p. 104). Others like Judith Orloff and Wayne Dyer have made the knowledge accessible to the general populous through seminars and self-help resources. If you're thinking that this sounds "way out there," stick with me. Solving problems that are rooted in our emotions requires a bit of digging into the soul and the psyche. In the remainder of the chapter, helpful strategies for overcoming fear-based leadership, forged by the positive psychology movement, will be explored.

"Intention is a framework for the creation of ultimate reality. It's the building plans for reality" (Houston & Sokolow, 2006, p. 3). Yet many of us make the mistake of devising plans for our schools without taking the time to examine our intentions. Allow the time for some introspection to determine your intention—what your goal as an educator really is.

Begin by taking a minute to think about and identify your past intentions as a school leader. This may be a difficult task, as many of them could have been subconscious. They might include:

♦ Getting through the year with few parent complaints.
♦ Keeping your job.
♦ Providing a safe and nurturing environment in which children can learn.
♦ Making learning fun.

The first two are obviously lower in nature because they center on self-preservation. However, though the second two intentions are higher in nature

Opportunity for Reflection

Reflect on the nature of your intentions as a school leader. What have they been? Have they been higher or lower in nature?
What are the risks involved in committing to higher intentions?

and contributors to student success, they still won't serve to independently bolster student achievement. If getting better results so that our young people can have a brighter future is what you want—and I believe that's what we all must desire—then that must be your intention.

The Power of Intention

You can think of intention as the ripples of a stone skipping along the surface of a pond. Each time it touches the pond, the stone generates a series of ever-expanding concentric circles, and the sets of circles intersect and overlap at some point. The pattern created by intention is similar to the surface of the pond after the stone passes through, but because the medium is life and not water, the reverberations travel like light and do not lose strength as they contribute to the fabric of life. Most leaders do not have a strong enough appreciation of the power of intention as a force for shaping reality. (Houston & Sokolow, 2006, p. 3)

A few months ago, a network news outlet carried a story about a principal who was determined to save his school's football program, which had been threatened by budget cuts. Through months of collaborative problem-solving with local business owners and civic groups as well as creative fundraising ventures, the school garnered more than enough funding to save the program. There was even enough for brand new uniforms and other team supplies. When interviewed, the principal stated that he had been bound and determined to save football at his school, no matter what he had to do to make it happen. There was no other option.

The same can be true for student achievement. When you, as a principal, set the intention to increase student learning substantially, then your *everyday* thoughts and actions *will* support that intention. As a principal, once I set the intention to increase student achievement, making it come to fruition was my laser-like focus. It's what I thought about and what I talked about constantly—to anyone on staff who would listen. My intention was clear and I expected it to happen.

> The process of saying things out loud helps to clarify your thinking and state your intention clearly. When you speak it out loud, you're raising a posse. You're enlisting support and the aid of others, whether you mean to or not, simply by sharing it. You've brought those who hear you into the circle of intention at that point. (Houston & Sokolow, 2006, p. 7)

On one busy day, I met a secondary school principal who shared a table with me at a restaurant during a busy lunch hour. She was in town from Boston visiting family. As we talked about our current professional circumstances, she shared that student achievement at her school was stagnant, causing her to be at a loss for what to do. In the next breath, she expressed frustration with No Child Left Behind (NCLB), because it required her large population of low-income students to meet a proficiency standard. "I know they're not going to be able to do it and so do all my teachers. It's just not possible," she explained.

Unaware of the power of her thoughts, she had set a strong intention that her students would not meet standards. That stone had been tossed, and her students and staff were suffering the reverberations.

Many of us are unaware of unproductive beliefs that can impact our intentions. I can now identify many as I reflect on my time as a classroom teacher. As a teacher, when my grade-level team received the standardized test results for our fifth graders at the end of my first year of teaching, the numbers didn't mean that much to me. The students had scored approximately the same as they had the year before.

During the following school year, we didn't change much about what we taught or the way we taught it. Not surprisingly, we got results similar to the prior year. But something did change in the way we felt about those results. This time, instead of only receiving our school's results, we were able to view on a chart how our fifth graders achieved in comparison to the other fifth grades in the county. It was a rude awakening. Most of the schools were outperforming us, and we got news that our students were struggling in middle school, coming into sixth grade unprepared to meet the academic demands.

That information immediately changed our beliefs about the students' capabilities, raising our expectations for their future performance. My intention became to have my students perform at least as well as the students in neighboring schools. And that year they did. My team realized that we, as teachers, were holding students back due to our negative beliefs. So we began to change our beliefs, which led to changes in expectations and daily practice. Sometimes, limiting beliefs are what keep us from having powerful intentions.

Attention: You Get What You Think About

Increasing the attention you give to your intention raises the probability that it will come to fruition (Houston & Sokolow, 2006, p. 21). But if you allow yourself to be distracted by unproductive thoughts, generated in the middle brain (the emotional center), they can take on an energy of their own. According to Houston and Sokolow, "Worry is a form of attention" (p. 25).

Several years ago, my husband and I bought a house that increased my daily commute to just under an hour. We were both in love with the location and its proximity to close friends and family, but I was worried about the long commute. I had experienced some health issues in the past, and was concerned that a flare-up could make driving that distance difficult. Concerned is really the wrong verb here. To tell you the truth, I was terrified that I had made a horrible mistake. I spent my time obsessing about what I would do if my joints flared up and I couldn't drive to work. Would we have to sell the new house? Would I lose my job? Would my husband hate me? I was making plans as if the worst had already occurred.

Within a few months of the move, my joints began to swell and in a short time, I was barely able to walk, let alone drive. My ankles were swollen, red hot to the touch, and terribly painful. My husband had to drive me to work and pick me up each day. It took months to get the flare-up under control. And a significant part of getting healthy was changing my thinking. One day, a healthcare practitioner asked me, "What's been happening in your life lately? What's been on your mind?"

Houston and Sokolow (2006) state, "Your thoughts set up an energy field, and that field tends to attract like-minded energy" (p. 25). If you spend time thinking about something that you don't want to have happen, you could actually be increasing the probability of it taking place. On the other hand, if you think positively, you increase the chances of good things happening in your life (p. 25). Lisa Ramirez (2009) affirms this in her research: "We all affect eternity by our thought patterns, our words and our deeds. They emit energy fields that contribute to the fabric that is woven into the unfolding pattern of life" (p. 7–8).

The first truth I had to realize was that I had given my attention over to getting sick, giving it my total focus. I had expected it. Even though I didn't want the illness, that's where my attention was every day. In order to heal,

I had to set getting healthy as a new intention and then stop thinking about being sick. It was a matter of revamping the neural pathways in my brain, which I had allowed to get stuck in a cycle of fear. My limbic system had taken control of both my old brain and new brain, impairing all thoughts, decisions, and normal bodily functioning (Hill, 2008, p. 25–27).

It wasn't easy. During the day, I would catch myself giving attention to my pain, or thinking about how depressing it was to feel so bad. In these times, I redirected my thoughts to the new intention of being healthy and active. I'd even imagine myself being able to take long walks or garden. Within a short time, the pain and swelling began to decrease and I was on the mend.

You get what you think about. It's that simple. And it's true in school leadership. If you are in a school that has an issue with unwanted student behavior, and that's what you think and talk about day in and day out, more inappropriate behavior is what you'll get. Unknowingly, you will set an intention to lead a school fraught with behavior problems. This is why programs like assertive discipline are so unsuccessful in extinguishing negative behavior, while programs such as Positive Behavior Intervention are so effective in increasing appropriate behavior and reducing problem student behavior. The latter program focuses on, looks for, expects, and rewards positive student behavior. Teachers and other staff members stay on the lookout for good behavior, which they teach and reward with verbal praise as well as tickets that can earn students prizes and privileges. They intend to have good behavior in their classrooms and give their attention to that end. Teachers do not spend time focused on negative behavior and how to punish it. I'm not suggesting here that cultivating positive learning behavior should be the primary focus of school leaders' attention, as it alone will not substantially increase learning. The message is: set your intention and then devote your full attention and energy to it. Always remember that you are likely to get whatever it is you allow yourself to think about, whether it is positive or negative in nature.

Resistant Thoughts

Deepak Chopra once stated that a belief is just a thought you think over and over again. So we can either live our lives filled with confidence and optimism or with fear and dread, depending on the contents of our everyday thoughts. Remember, "negative emotions are linked to survival—and are much stronger" (Hill, 2008, p. 29). Moreover, if you've been unconsciously thinking negative thoughts over a period of time, these unproductive beliefs may have created actual changes in the brain: emotions affect thoughts affect emotions. So how do we break the cycle? We break it through mental interventions.

Mental activity changes neural activity, and neural activity leads to changes in neural structure: *Neurons that fire together, wire together.* . . . Therefore, a person can use her mind to change her brain to change her mind. (Hanson, 2010, p. 6)

When you find yourself feeling down or fearful, think about what you've been thinking about! Try to identify the individual thoughts causing the negative feelings. These resistant thoughts are usually untruths that, if left unchecked, can torpedo a positive intention to improve student learning. Figure 2.1 shows several examples that did their best to monopolize my thoughts as a school leader.

FIGURE 2.1. Thought Scaffold

Resistant Thought	*Aligned Thought*
My students performing below grade level will not be able to meet grade level standards no matter what we do.	With some simple yet meaningful changes in classroom instruction, even my lower performing students will make accelerated progress, meeting grade level standards.
My teachers won't be willing to change their instructional practices. They are already so overwhelmed and overworked.	With my support and confidence, teachers will begin to see the direct relationship between instructional change and increased student achievement. Efficacy will then be contagious!
My staff will hate me if I hold them accountable for student achievement.	Teachers may at first react negatively, but morale will improve as they see me being a true partner with them and as their sense of pride grows when student learning begins to improve.

Remember that in order to lead others in the courageous journey of improving your school, you must keep your intention in the forefront of your mind and keep watch over your thoughts to make sure they are in alignment with the goal.

Facing Your Fear

Committing to the higher intention of ensuring greater levels of student learning doesn't mean that your old fears will magically disappear. There will still be times when your brain's limbic system will take over and you'll fear failure, rejection, judgment, and purposelessness. Although few would admit to it, this is one of the reasons that many school leaders choose to set low expectations of what can be accomplished. Low expectations equal low disappointment. But if we settle for this, we behave like hamsters on a wheel—working hard every day and getting nowhere. There is no reward in the work. The antidote to this fear is the hope of truly fulfilling our ultimate professional need for self-worth. This only comes with student success.

The truth is, when you intend to increase student learning in your school, your fears are sure to increase for a time. It only makes sense that if we raise the bar for our performance, our teachers' performance, and our students' performance, there is more room for failure. There are also more opportunities to face rejection and judgment from both teachers and parents. Then throw in your own critical voice that will try to convince you that your new intention is unachievable, and will ultimately make you look like a fool. Thoughts like these are considered resistant thoughts because they work against your positive intention, zapping your confidence and energy.

Be vigilant. When you catch yourself feeling down or afraid, take a thought inventory to identify the negative or resistant ones, and adjust them. The goal here is to take a situation in which you would normally fold to anxiety, making a fear-based decision, and instead choose to make a fearless decision. I don't mean fearless in its literal sense here—without fear. Instead, I suggest using the new brain to implement the following steps.

1. Acknowledge the feeling of fear. Remind yourself that it's normal to be afraid.
2. Remind yourself of the higher concerns at stake.
3. Identify resistant thoughts that block your intention. Make mental adjustments.
4. Move forward in confidence and take action to increase student learning.

Opportunity for Reflection

What has been the focus of your attention lately? Reflect on a time when you got what you gave your attention to, whether positive or negative.

Reflect upon your daily thought patterns. What negative or resistant thoughts can you identify? How can they be adjusted to support your intention?

In *Conquering Fear*, Harold Kushner (2009) reminds us, "Our goal should not be the total absence of fear but the mastery of fear, being the master of our emotions rather than their slave" (p. 11). Developing courage entails feeling fear that should be feared, but enduring it for moral reasons. Short-circuit the direct pathway from you middle brain (emotions) to your old brain (decision-making). Free yourself to engage your new brain (rational thought) before making a decision. So when these fears arise, remind yourself what's at stake and that it is of far greater significance to strive to substantially increase your students' competencies rather than to play it safe in order to preserve your ego. The consequences of mediocrity far outweigh the risks of high expectations.

But getting better results demands systemic changes throughout the school. The way you do business each and every day cannot stay the same. Everyone will have to work outside their comfort zones. In order to prepare your staff for change, the first requirement is building trusting relationships. According to Hultman (1998), "Trust helps foster readiness to change, whereas mistrust fosters resistance to change" (p. 151). So as well as addressing personal fears, it is essential that a school leader identify and address teacher fears, which equal teacher pain. This process begins by building trust.

Build Trust

When I think of the leaders I've been able to trust over the years, they were all genuine people who weren't afraid to be themselves around me. Moreover, I could depend on them to be there to lead, day in and day out. Hultman (1998) echoes this view in his explanation of how we decide whether or not to put our trust in someone:

We evaluate their behavior according to its consistency and sincerity. Consistency has to do with whether or not the other person is ethical, reliable, and dependable. Sincerity has to do with whether or not the other person is genuine and nonmanipulative. . . . Trust demands both consistency and sincerity; one without the other won't do. We need to believe the other person not only will do the right thing but will do it for the right reasons. (p. 152)

As leaders, these two elements go to the core of who we are and point to our commitments and motivations. If we are motivated by self-centered concerns such as popularity, acceptance, power, or control, our actions will give us up, causing others to mistrust us. It will not work to try *acting* in a consistent and sincere manner. You simply can't fake it. That's why it is imperative to make a commitment to higher concerns versus lower concerns before moving forward.

I'll never forget an emotionally-charged incident that occurred with a particular teacher. The principal and I, the assistant principal, had decided to move one of our best teachers from one grade level to another. The reasons for the move included student enrollment numbers, as well as her valuable expertise that would have benefitted the other grade-level team. When we talked to the teacher about our plan, she reacted strongly, obviously angry with our idea—but it's what she said that will stay with me. Pointing at the principal, she accused, "I know why you're really doing this. You don't think I know what this is really about?"

Both the principal and I were shocked and confused by her reaction. We asked her politely to fill us in on the "real" reason, but she refused. Within weeks, she had transferred to another school. It was a loss for our students. To this day, neither of us knows the nefarious reason that she thought drove our decision. But that's not the point. The point is that even though our motivations were pure, she didn't believe they were. And that's what mattered—we were mistrusted. We had failed to show a pattern over time of being consistent and sincere. This incident forced me to take the time to examine my own past motivations and actions, which could have contributed to her lack of trust.

Be Who You Are

If you visit a bookstore today and investigate the section devoted to leadership and management, I can guarantee you'll find a slew of books that list *the* characteristics of an effective leader. These authors must believe that their readers can change their personality traits at will in order to fit the caricature of the perfect principal. I reject this notion in favor of one that is inclusive of many different styles and personal qualities. One essential element to building trust with school staff is the principal's ability to be vulnerable and authentic. In other words, it's about the ability to function as your authentic self, rather than hiding behind a professional persona that feebly embodies the latest "top ten characteristics of a leader." The practice of taking on personas is a defensive maneuver executed out of fear—fear of rejection. It provides a protective shell that keeps people from getting too close, from finding out too much. Though the protection they provide is ultimately damaging to the trusting relationships between you and your staff.

You see, in order to earn trust you must first offer trust. I know this is a scary prospect—offering trust to people who you may not know very well and who may very well wish ill of you. Even so, make the conscious choice to remove your protective shell, thus allowing those around you to know the real you. If beneath the persona, they find someone with higher concerns, then trust will build. They don't need to find an oracle. In fact, finding a regular person with some limitations in skill and knowledge is perfect—because it's real.

So why do many school leaders feel the need to be all-knowing in the eyes of their teachers? Kevin Cashman (1997), a leadership consultant, recalls an experience with just this type of leader:

> I remember working with an executive who believed, because he was at the top of the organization, he must always have all the answers, and that if he revealed any limitations others would perceive him as weak and inadequate. Eventually, in his need to always be 'right,' he made several errors and brought his organization to a crisis. With our coaching, he used the crisis to break from his old pattern. He faced up to his troops, acknowledged his mistakes, and asked for their help. His co-workers were shocked, but they rushed to his support and enthusiastically resolved the crisis.*

School leaders should admit to not having all the answers. When leaders admit their limitations, teachers can too. This is liberating for everyone and frees up teachers to be learners instead of knowers. By functioning in this manner, leaders can allow themselves to be real and authentic. But be careful here. Admitting to not having all the answers does not mean accepting failure

*From Cashman, Authentic Leadership. *Innovative Leader,* 6(11). Copyright 2006 Winston J. Brill & Associates. Reprinted with permission from Winston J. Brill & Associates.

or mediocrity in your school. This is where synergy comes into play. You must believe that together, with your leadership team, problems that were unsolvable by each individual will be solved through collaborative energy, creativity, and commitment.

Commit to Open Communication

Another vital part of being authentic is facilitating open communication. In many cases, complex educational issues cannot be solved unless people are willing to speak about uncomfortable topics. I call this speaking about the unspeakable. Many topics have only become uncomfortable because of institutionalized beliefs that develop a closed culture within a school. But if school leaders muster the courage to "go there"—the place no one else will go, I assure you that others will gladly follow. It will liberate the group.

One difficult issue I had to face as an administrator was why daily instruction didn't align to state and local curriculum. At a meeting with school improvement members, I asked team leaders to show how they planned for their daily instruction. They dropped heavy curriculum binders onto the table and began going through them with me. I saw hundreds of benchmarks and learning outcomes in each heavy binder, so I asked, "You take these binders home regularly and use them to plan from?"

Silence.

So I followed up with, "I think it would be difficult to plan for instruction with such a volume of benchmarks. It doesn't look easy."

That was all it took. The team leaders then easily spoke about their struggles in planning for daily instruction using the broad information provided in the curriculum documents. At the end of our two hour conversation, we had decided on a plan of action to make the planning process easier for teachers. A concise planning guide that identified the specific reading outcomes expected at each grade level, broken down by quarter, was developed. We combined objectives where we could to make the document short and manageable. That was the first step necessary in aligning our instruction with the curriculum. And it wouldn't have been possible without being real about the daily lives of teachers.

I believe most teachers are already aware of the actions they need to take in order to optimize student learning. But the obstacles of daily life can get in the way of those needed actions. This is true for many aspects of our daily lives. For example, I know that I should weed my garden for just a few minutes each day. If I were to follow through with this plan, the weeding would be manageable and my garden would look presentable. Instead, the demands of daily life thwart my best intentions—dinner must be made, errands run, laundry put away. Before I know it, darkness has set in and I end the day feeling like a failure for not completing a simple five-minute task. Our teachers can feel the same way about many aspects of their responsibilities. But rarely will they admit to having these issues for fear of judgment. We need to listen to their struggles in a no-fault, non-judgmental way, and then work together to find doable solutions.

Support Teachers

When you set and share the intention to improve student learning, teachers will suddenly feel pressure to get results. To help alleviate some pressure, the drive to improve must be balanced by caring for teachers. If not, the school climate, which may already be suffering due to negative cultural norms or low self-perception, could suffer as staff feel the tremendous weight of higher expectations. School leaders must strive to make teachers' lives more livable. This can be accomplished through:

1. **Getting in the trenches.** We've all heard the adage, "You can't lead from your office." And it's true. Leaders have to get their hands dirty with teachers. There must be a practical partnership, which requires regular formal and informal conversations with teachers about student progress, as well as being present in classrooms to see first hand what students are learning and whether or not they master it. A principal needs to observe the implementation of instructional strategies that have been agreed upon by the team in order to give feedback and encouragement. Since teachers cannot readily watch one another teach, a building leader can provide needed information regularly as to differences in style and technique so that variations in student achievement from class to class can be better understood and attributed to specific teacher actions. Finally, when students fail to learn, leaders should be connected enough to help teams determine appropriate next steps. Taking these actions breaks down the invisible barrier between principal and teacher and puts everyone on the same team in shared accountability.

2. **Protecting teachers' time.** If gone unchecked, too much of a teacher's day can be taken up by issues that have little to do with student achievement. Returning emails, planning for non-academic school/community events, handling fundraiser information and money, and dealing with attendance, lunch, and recess issues can quickly dominate precious minutes of planning time. Find ways to minimize or streamline administrative tasks, while

Opportunity for Reflection

What are some unhealthy expectations you've had for your teachers? Where did these expectations originate? What will you do to communicate healthy expectations?

What is the current state of trust between you and your staff? What have you done to weaken trust? What steps will you take this week to strengthen trust?

protecting or increasing time to collaboratively analyze data, plan instruction, and problem-solve. I suggest using time already allotted in the school calendar (e.g. faculty meetings, professional development days), as well as substitute time to accomplish this important work.

3. Encouraging teachers to keep a healthy balance between work life and home life. Too often, school leaders unknowingly send damaging messages to teachers about how they should use the 24 hours in each day. Teachers who spend 12 hours a day at school are highly regarded, spoken about in glowing terms, while those who leave at their contracted time may be looked down upon. Instead of passing judgment, we need to help teachers find ways to be successful within a reasonable workday, so they may go home at a decent hour and have quality time with family and friends. If this doesn't happen, not only will many schools remain negative places to work, I predict that teachers will leave the profession at faster rates than they do now. As a building leader, keep a realistic view of life as a teacher and work to improve the quality of their professional lives within your school. This will go a long way to developing real trust with teachers.

The remainder of this book will focus upon six vital decisions that must be made by administrators, decisions that will either propel schools forward or halt progress, depending on how they are made. But these decisions that can hasten real improvement are often times risky and, therefore, must be given serious consideration before action is taken. Each chapter describes the decision at hand, why many leaders allow fear to influence their decisions, and most importantly, how to make a fearless decision. Fearless decisions overcome institutional, social, and personal pressures to create schools that ensure high levels of achievement for all.

3

Fearless Decision: Dealing with Conflict

Imagine it is Thanksgiving Day. After hours of travel, you arrive at your destination, ready to reconnect with and enjoy extended family. After joyous hellos and hugs, everyone gathers for dinner, passing dishes and catching up on the happenings in one another's lives. This happy buzz continues until Uncle Ted makes an insensitive comment to a cousin. The table quiets, and then slowly returns to its pre-missile strike status. The comment has been ignored and goodwill predominates once again—that is, until Uncle Ted chooses a new target.

The pattern continues, which probably explains why at each holiday, fewer family members attend the gathering. By avoiding conflict with Ted, peace is preserved for the holiday meal at hand. But long-term, his assault tears the family apart.

The same pattern of conflict avoidance can be seen in our everyday professional lives as well. For example, every school leader has the classroom that is more difficult to enter than all the rest. It is stealthily avoided during regular school walk-throughs, the inside seen mainly during the obligatory formal observation. Why don't we go into the classroom? Because we know that we'll see something unacceptable. It could be inappropriate student behavior due to the teacher's ineffective classroom management practices. It could be students failing to learn due to the teacher's lack of planning or lack of content/pedagogical knowledge. Whatever the disaster, we know it will require major intervention on our part to make it right—intervention that will spark conflict. So, with a sigh of relief, we pass this classroom and preserve peace for the day. Peace that comes at the expense of students who aren't learning.

Throughout history though, there have been those willing to greet, even create, conflict for the good of the order. Take Rosa Parks. When she refused to give up her seat on the bus that day in 1955, she surely had a sense of the storm of controversy that would ensue. Parks and many others like her helped change the hearts and minds of America. Personal gain and even safety was put aside, and conflict was used strategically to help facilitate social justice. Had she taken the easy path and given her seat to the white passenger, I don't believe the civil rights movement would have gained the needed momentum at the time. Her action was one of the touchstones that propelled the civil rights movement and spurred needed legislation.

So if we know the high cost of avoiding conflict, why does it happen every day in schools across this country? First let me begin with an important disclaimer. Some conflict can and should be avoided. Conflict for the sake of conflict is not wise or healthy and will not help better your school. A principal's role is not to go barreling around the building, looking for a fight. What we are exploring here are the tough situations that find you, even in your best hiding places, and demand that you respond—for the good of students and for the health of the organization.

In this chapter, we will focus on those incidents that, if faced, provide unique opportunities for your school to grow. If ignored, however, these same situations have the power to fester, infect, and stunt the growth and effectiveness of the school.

So, back to the question at hand: Why do we avoid these conflicts when we know that facing them head-on is the best course of action? The answer takes us back to our biology. Since the old brain is self-centered and concerned with its own survival above all else, it is highly interested in solutions that will alleviate any pain it is feeling (Renvoise & Morin, 2007, p. 20). Remember that fear is a very powerful form of emotional pain. Therefore, the administrator who walks past the troubled classroom alleviates the fear and pain associated with facing a situation that will cause tension and conflict. As Wright reminds us, "genetically we're designed for self-preservation. Goals high on the list for human beings are feeling good about ourselves and accruing allies" (qtd. in Hill, 2008, p. 23).

Need for Respect vs. Fear of Judgment

In order to address important problems, principals will have to take a stand on issues—clearly communicate their points of view on expectations, such as:

- Planning
- Instructional delivery
- Classroom management
- Interpersonal relationships
- Professionalism

If school leaders aren't confident enough in their professional knowledge and beliefs to greet dissenting opinions with openness and ease, the fear of judgment will trigger avoidance behavior. The need for the respect of teachers could drive leaders to align their beliefs with those of the majority of the staff. Instead of leading the school, the principal ends up following in order to have his actions perceived as ethical and just. But the most successful leaders have continuous, honest internal dialogue, which helps keep them aligned with their true vision and increases their ability to get others on board (Scott, 2004, p. 9–10).

One principal described an experience that tested her ability to stand strong under judgment while tackling teacher quality. Concerned about one teacher's planning and instructional delivery after unfavorable observations, she required the teacher to plan daily instruction with a mentor teacher and turn in those plans weekly. Several staff members who worked closely with this teacher began to treat the principal differently. It was clear that her relationship with them was strained due to their perceptions about the actions she had taken. One staff member finally shared with her that he didn't feel it was fair to ask any teacher for lesson plans. He went on to state that making a tenured teacher plan with a mentor was inappropriate and bordered on harassment. The principal's character was definitely in question.

She thanked him for sharing his point-of-view and assured him that her actions were motivated by the best interests of students. Still, it took months for the involved staff members to begin to trust and respect her once again. She continued to earn that trust by aligning all of her actions with what she believed to be best for students and being transparent in her thinking and decision making. If she had a strong fear of judgment, this principal may have decided not to face this teacher who wasn't meeting standards in her planning and instructional delivery. It certainly would have been easier to turn a blind eye and act as if the teacher were doing a good job.

Need for Acceptance vs. Fear of Rejection

As school leaders, our faculty and staff become like a second family to us. In fact, we probably spend more time with them than we do with some of our real family members. We care for them, worry about them, and support them through both professional and personal challenges. But if leaders aren't careful, these positive relationships can keep us from leading in the way we need to. When we begin to care more about being liked and accepted by our faculty and staff than we do about making the right decisions for students, then the fear of rejection has clouded our judgment. This need for social acceptance is what causes new teachers to strive to be their students' friend and what causes insecure parents to strive to be their children's buddy.

Opportunity for Reflection

What conflicts have you avoided as a school leader?
Which need (respect, acceptance) most impacts your ability to face conflict?

One secondary principal dealt with this fear when he insisted on closer supervision of students in the hallways between classes. Because of changes in the school schedule and in the policy for reporting student progress, teacher workload had increased. The faculty was feeling overworked and looked for ways to increase their own efficiency, as well as take mental breaks during the day. The solution for many was to use the few minutes between classes to catch up on administrative tasks in their classroom or just take a moment of downtime for themselves. Unfortunately, this left the hallways largely unsupervised and allowed an unsafe environment for students. As he prepared to speak to the teachers about the situation, he felt his own anxiety begin to surface. He saw their exhaustion and understood their feelings regarding increased workload. The teachers would be angry with his request that they be visible in the hallways, viewing the demand as uncaring toward their situation. While he ended up making the right decision for students, causing some strife and conflict, this incident shed light on the natural longing for a favorable reception from staff.

So, with the reality that the respect and acceptance of school staff are important for any principal, how can the fear of judgment and rejection be overcome in order to deal with necessary conflict effectively?

Antidote: Develop the Courage to Welcome Healthy Conflict

Set Your Intention

Recognize the fear when it comes. Don't ignore it or push it down into the unconscious. Allow yourself to feel it. Does it lodge in your stomach? Your chest? Or perhaps in your back? Just be with it for a few minutes. Don't run from it or distract yourself. Remind yourself that it may be uncomfortable, but it won't kill you and it will dissipate. Then, to move past the fear, remind yourself of why you have chosen to be a school leader. If your answer is to improve student learning, then immediately the focus is shifted from you to the student. This movement is crucial when changing thinking from lower, self-centered concerns to higher, student-centered concerns.

Start to reframe the way you think about conflict. This will, in turn, positively impact your emotions. Welcome healthy conflict as proof that your organization continues to grow and improve. Carl Jung (1960) once stated, "The most intense conflicts, if overcome, leave behind a sense of security and calm which is not easily disturbed . . . it is just these intense conflicts and their conflagration which are needed in order to produce valuable and lasting results" (p. 26). When faculty and staff are being their authentic selves—sharing their opinions with you—and you are doing the same, conflict is a natural occurrence. Conflict is one product of healthy communication and necessary to make progress together. Hultman (1998) identifies three stages of development that all organizations go through—The Three Cs: Courtesy, Conflict, and Cohesiveness (p. 159).

> During the first stage, people are polite and diplomatic with each other, as fear inhibits open expression. In the second stage, anger, frustration, and resentment break through the fear, as issues dividing people begin to surface. Anger is a more productive emotion than fear, because it can serve as a catalyst for positive energy. In the third stage, people bind together. (Hultman, 1998, p. 159)

The points-of-view at the heart of conflict are beliefs that affect the school every day and, if uncovered and openly discussed, can propel the organization forward. The problem is that most of the time they remain unspoken, contaminating the school culture with suppressed negativity. It shouldn't be the spoken disputes that scare us; it should be what's unspoken. Making the unspoken spoken begins with you.

Find Your Voice

Being willing to speak what you normally keep inside requires us to muster the courage to tell the truth.

> [I]n the workplace, and in our conversations with ourselves, we'd like to tell the truth. We'd like to be able to successfully tackle the topic that's keeping us stuck or apart, but . . . we don't know how to avoid the all-too-familiar outcome of talks gone south, and besides, we've learned to live with it. Why wreck another meeting with our colleagues . . . trying to resolve the tough issues or answer the big questions? We're tired and we just want peace in the land. The problem is, whether you are running an organization or your life, you

are required to be responsive to your world. And that response often requires change. We effect change by engaging in robust conversations with ourselves and others. (Scott, 2004, p. 6–7)

Susan Scott (2004) identifies these important exchanges that foster positive change as fierce conversations:

In its simplest form, a fierce conversation is one in which we come out from behind ourselves into the conversation and make it real. . . . Fierce conversations are about moral courage, clear requests, and taking action. Fierce is an attitude. A way of conducting business. A way of leading. A way of life. (p. 7, 10)

Start small. Don't try to make an overnight change. Begin by being present in your everyday conversations with a commitment to sharing real thoughts and ideas. Work up to the situations you know will be highly-charged and emotional. You'll find that changing these small conversations will begin to develop your confidence.

At one school, an opportunity arose that gave administrators the chance to practice fierce conversations centered upon professional judgment and trust. At the end of every school year, language arts teachers reported the final reading level for each of their students on the articulation card. These were the levels at which next year's teacher was to begin reading instruction for each child.

But it never actually worked out that way. Instead, when the new school year began, reading teachers would reassess each student to find the appropriate beginning reading level. When asked why they did this, teachers responded that the recommended reading levels were never accurate and, therefore, couldn't be trusted. So reassessment continued, taking weeks of valuable instructional time *and* causing a disruptive shuffling of students around to different groups and classes. Tensions built between grade-level teachers, fostering an uncooperative "us against them" mindset. It was a situation that had been ignored for far too long.

The administrators knew it was time to resolve this issue, so they brought the problem to their leadership team, hoping they might simply talk through it. But upon broaching the topic, the teachers around the table averted eye contact, lowered their heads, sunk into their seats—trying their best to disappear.

Unsure of what else to do, but too stubborn to drop the subject, the administrators began to share the assessment problem as they saw it, along with their concerns about its detrimental effects on students and staff. They urged the team to just get real and put everything out on the table—that they were all smart and caring enough to wade through it all to find a positive solution.

After opening up to them, the principal then threw out the first question, and stunningly, the teachers began to open up too. Some of the questions and comments raised during the conversation were:

"So, why *don't* we just go by last year's teacher's recommendation?"

"That *would* allow us to get right into instruction, which would be great!"

"But that's not fair to students, who will have either gained or lost skills over the summer."

"Wouldn't we be able to see that when we started teaching our reading groups and then just make adjustments as needed?"

"I think so. Besides, students who have lost some skill over the summer usually pick back up pretty quickly."

"Yeah, but we all know it's not just that. We don't want to say it, but the issue here is that last year's teacher's recommendations are always wrong."

"Well, they're not *always* wrong."

"But they're wrong enough that we can't trust them."

"Okay, so why are they wrong at all?"

"Because doing running records is a subjective process and everyone does them differently. I mean, we were all trained at different times and different points in our careers. We all think we're doing them right and everyone else is doing them wrong."

"So, what can we do about that?"

"Do we need consistent training in how to give a running record?"

"Yes, but I think some teachers will be offended by that if we do it. They'll think they don't need it."

"That's okay. They can think it's for everyone else's benefit."

"It's been a long time since we were all trained together and heard the same message. I think it would cut down on a lot of the variations we're seeing."

"Could our reading specialist train everyone together during a faculty meeting or other common time?"

"Yeah, I think we should do that."

"But that's not the only issue. There will still be teachers who struggle to use the assessment accurately. We need some sort of system of quality control."

"Could the reading specialist do some random spot checks? Like could she pull a few students from different classes, give them the alternate running record to get an instructional level, and then compare it to what the classroom teacher reported out?"

"Oh, I'm not sure how that would go over."

"But it wouldn't be a gotcha. It would be a helpful way of making sure we're all being consistent. If I was doing it wrong, I'd want someone to tell me!"

Opportunity for Reflection

Reflect on the conversations you have in your school. What discussions or topics are comfortable for you? What topics have you been avoiding?

When was the last time you said something that was real and true for you? What happens to the conversation when you are willing to get show your authentic self?

"Well, we'd have to present that to the staff in a very sensitive way. But I think everyone would get on board with it if it meant less assessing for everyone in the beginning of the year."

"*And* if it meant that we could *trust* the levels that went on the articulation cards."

Once the true issues were out in the open, the discussion gained momentum and the administrators knew the team would work through them successfully. In her book *Fierce Conversations*, leadership development architect Susan Scott (2004) writes, "When the conversation is real, the change occurs before the conversation has even ended" (p. 8). The conversation continued until all were comfortable with a plan of action to address the problem. A discussion that had been so uncomfortable in the beginning ended up energizing everyone around the table with hope and optimism. According to Scott, "A fierce conversation is like the first parachute jump from an airplane. In anticipation, you perspire and your mouth goes dry. Once you've left the plane, it's an adrenaline rush that is indescribable" (p. 11).

The leadership team was able to confidently present the issue and action plan to their grade-level teams, get feedback, and implement a solution that would help immediately. Even better, it would also provide for increased professional skill and more trusting relationships among teachers over the long-term. This fierce conversation had transformed a conflict into a positive outcome for the school as a whole.

Build Trust

Hultman (1998) writes, "It's essential for people to learn that they can handle conflict; otherwise they never fully trust each other" (p. 159). Being real and speaking the truth will go a long way in building trust with faculty and staff.

But having a leader who welcomes conflict instead of squelching or avoiding it can be confusing for teachers. Along with the trust-building strategies described in Chapter 2, using a conflict transformation paradigm for approaching disagreements and teaching that paradigm to staff will help to build trust within the school. Conflict transformation, an idea and movement brought about by John Paul Lederach (2003), goes beyond conflict management and conflict resolution to view conflict as a positive tool that can change those involved in it for the better:

> A transformational approach begins with pro-active foundations: 1) a positive orientation toward conflict and 2) a willingness to engage in the conflict in an effort to produce constructive change or growth. While conflict often produces long-standing cycles of hurt and destruction, the key to transformation is the capacity to envision conflict as having potential for constructive change.

When utilizing this approach, school leaders must commit to being directly involved with staff to engage with and support them during times of strife and discord. Be in it with them. Be positive. And be willing to be changed.

Campaign and Show Clear Contrast

As you begin to live out a conflict transformation approach at work, it will help to promote the idea to your staff by appealing to the old brain. First, identify teachers' current **pain**. In this case, it is most likely that they exist in a work environment that frowns upon any conflict. They are probably accustomed to leaders who perceive all conflict as bad; therefore, they avoid it. Those who wish to air differences of opinion and work through them are identified as troublemakers. But it doesn't have to be that way. Instead of being a leader who buries his head in the sand when things get dicey, really listen to teachers and handle conflict confidently.

The **gain** for teachers in a conflict transformation environment is a welcoming of different opinions and a willingness to face challenges. Teachers do not have to be afraid to voice real concerns. And they'll know that when they do, they won't be ignored by leadership. They'll be heard. It is just that infusion of ideas that energizes and strengthens the organization, making it a stimulating place to work, learn and grow.

To show the contrast, share that you will not hide when conflict arises, forcing teachers to fend for themselves during difficult situations. Instead, tell your faculty—and then show them—that you will be there, ready to help.

Opportunity for Reflection

Reflect on a current problem or issue in your school. How can a conflict transformation approach help you to handle it differently than you normally would?

How will you show staff that you are willing to deal with important problems and listen to varying opinions?

Take Action

If so far, this chapter has left you imagining you and your staff holding hands around a campfire, singing kumbaya, then it's time to amend the picture with a measured dose of reality.

Be courageous! Don't avoid difficult conversations with faculty and staff because you can't get a quick win. While the long-term outcome for fierce conversations done well is positive for students and for the school, they can leave some discord in the short-term. Not every conflict or problem will be transformed into an immediate positive for all. So, start small. Begin by being honest in your one-on-one conversations with teachers.

At one point, a secondary school administrator had a teacher in his school who was struggling—really struggling. She had trouble with classroom management, planning, and instruction. All of her walk-throughs and observations detailed specific actions she needed to take in order to continue teaching. She worked with a mentor, took advantage of all the supports that had put into place for her, and expended more than adequate effort to improve. But she wasn't improving. Not only that, but she looked miserable and absolutely exhausted all the time. Finally, during a post-observation conference, the principal leveled with her by asking, "Is this really what you want to do for the next 30 years? You just don't look very happy." She broke down in tears. Until that moment, she hadn't allowed herself to consider that her calling might be somewhere else, doing something quite different. Although she left the principal's office that day troubled, the conversation had opened the door for her to think bigger about her life and her choices. She eventually left teaching to pursue a career in a field that she loved and in which she was naturally gifted.

Don't tolerate unacceptable behavior. In any organization, there are folks who test the patience of both leadership and their co-workers. Their motivation is not to better the organization, but instead, to spread negative energy.

Often times, these people carry around emotional hurts from past and present professional and personal experiences, making them and those around them miserable. Even when leaders try to meet these staff members' emotional needs, it isn't enough to overcome the long-term damage that's been done to the person's patterns of thinking and reacting to others. Since our role is not that of a psychologist, we focus on what we can do to promote positive behavior. Setting and consistently reinforcing clear expectations for conduct goes a long way to ensuring a constructive work environment. Hultman (1998) writes, "People often test the lower limits of behavior to see if the leader is serious about the standards. A leader who insists on positive behavior gains respect, while a leader who ignores negative behavior loses respect" (p. 157).

In one secondary school, a teacher's behavior was ignored at the cost of the rest of the team. The team leader reported to the administration that a teacher on her team had been refusing to attend team meetings, use common assessments, plan with the team, or discuss student achievement data. He was acting, instead, as an independent contractor. This behavior was not a part of the school's values or expectations. When the administration confronted the teacher about his behavior, he became indignant, even borderline insubordinate. He was an experienced bully. The administration was unprepared for this kind of reaction, and after talking him down, doubted the wisdom of their decision to approach him. They viewed it as causing conflict instead of healing it. The team soon surmised that the administration would not be getting involved in the situation again. So the team leader and a fellow team member moved to other grade levels. And the rest of the teachers gave up on having a functional team. The uncooperative teacher stayed put, knowing he had found a place that would tolerate his negative behavior.

> Behavior is so crucial to a group's success or failure that willingness to abide by . . . norms should be a qualification for membership. Making this expectation nonnegotiable sends a strong message ("If you want to work with me, this is what I need from you"). Thus, when people refuse to abide by the expectations, they are deciding not to be in the group. Members allowed to remain in spite of their behavior will undermine team morale and performance—you may win the battle, but you'll lose the war. (Hultman, 1998, p. 157)*

Don't allow cliques to control school dynamics. Most schools experience the results of cliques or subgroups at one time or another. These groups develop more often in a work environment going through the change process—for

*From Hultman, Ken, *Making Change Irresistible.* Copyright 1998 Davies-Black Publishing. Copyright 2005 Ken Hultman. Reprinted with permission of the author.

instance, a principal who sets a new intention to significantly increase student learning. Dan Hill (2008) describes the four groups, or types of workers, that usually exist during significant workplace change.

- **The winners:** Those employees most likely to benefit from organizational change and to feel pride at the prospect of an enhanced company identity.
- **The switchers:** These high achievers can readily go elsewhere, and may not have the patience for the turmoil and paralysis that comes with change.
- **The survivors:** Employees who will do anything to hold on, for reasons varying from trying to protect a pension to lacking the energy or talent to go elsewhere.
- **The losers:** Those badly affected by the change may turn into the walking dead because of a loss of hope combined with increased fear or even anger. They can harm the winners, motivate the switchers to go and make the survivors even more bitter. (p. 275–6)

When you begin to change the culture by prioritizing student achievement, teachers who have a sense of efficacy will make up the "winners" group. They will support and even design new initiatives and most likely become your aspiring leaders. Their positive energy will be extremely valuable during the change process. But winners are more than just yes men. Their desire to succeed and courage to defy the status quo will sometimes challenge school leaders and propel the school forward.

Your "switchers" will communicate very little with you or others. They will quietly choose not to stay and put forth the energy necessary to withstand the transition, even if they believe in it. Switchers will only hurt morale in that their leaving shows non-support of leadership and the new changes.

The "survivors" usually don't believe in the changes happening in the school, but are determined to do whatever it takes to keep their positions. They try to fly under the radar of leadership, changing as little as possible about their day-to-day work activities in order to fit in with new expectations. They can sometimes be brought along by the winners and end up being very successful in the new working environment.

And then there are the "losers." These are the teachers who know they lack the professional skill necessary to succeed under the new expectations of high student achievement. They don't believe that focusing on student learning is fair to them and frequently complain of leaders having unrealistic expectations. Forming powerful cliques within the school, these teachers commiserate together, and at their worst, plot the downfall of school leaders.

Opportunity for Reflection

What topics at work make you uncomfortable or likely to avoid conversation? What would happen if you were willing to discuss them?

What cliques or subgroups are exerting themselves in your school right now? What feeling or sentiment is banding them together? What actions can you take to bring them along? What toxic elements are you trying to ignore?

Hill (2008) believes them to be so harmful, he states, "this group must be removed from the company ranks as quickly as possible to avoid infecting others with their negativity" (p. 276). This isn't always so easy in the world of public schools, but I believe it is well worth it to trudge through the required red tape in order to rid the school of toxic elements. Once one of these teachers leaves the school, either on his or her own accord or through administrative action, the others will follow closely behind. And the negative cliques they've formed will disband and dissolve.

One high school principal described a situation in which he decided to deal with a toxic teacher. She was an ineffective instructor who refused help and support and knew that she would eventually be let go through progressive discipline. Instead of facing the fact that teaching probably wasn't the right fit for her and her strengths, she plotted reprisal on the school administration. Accusing the administration of harassment, she harnessed the power of her cliques and campaigned throughout the school staff, then central office and the school community for the removal of the principal. The principal was forced to undergo a formal human resources investigation, and after months of interviews and meetings, was deemed innocent. In the end, the teacher was transferred to another school in the district and the principal got to stay. Although it was a harrowing experience, this principal wouldn't have changed a thing about what he did. Likening it to ripping off a band-aid, he stated that it was worth going through acute emotional pain for a short time rather than deal with her hurting students at his school for years to come. The result broke the stronghold of this teacher's clique on the school's climate and culture. When negative cliques are confronted consistently over time, they either leave the organization or dissolve.

4

Fearless Decision: Taking Action to Impact Student Learning

When I was a kid, our next door neighbor was Mr. Al, or as I liked to call him, Mr. Owl—as if he were a character in one of the Frog and Toad books. (Embarrassingly, I really did think that was his name.) His back yard was the cut-through we used to get to a friend's house, so we saw him almost every day sitting on a lawn chair reading *Consumer Reports*. He was always researching his next big purchase. There was the car, the dishwasher, the freezer. The trouble was he never actually bought anything. Just as he would zero in on a final choice, the models would change, spurring him to start the entire selection process all over again. He never took action.

In this chapter, three common situations that keep schools from taking action will be explored: paralysis by analysis, the indecisive school improvement team, and the school improvement dissertation. Root causes will then be identified and solutions provided through school improvement structure and processes.

Paralysis by Analysis

When I began my teaching career, we would complain that we had very limited information upon which to make instructional decisions. There was an end-of-year state performance assessment that measured grade-level performance as a whole, but failed to provide individual student scores. Then there was a norm-referenced assessment that did not align with our curriculum, but did provide individual results. The only other data we had to work with was the information provided by our periodic teacher-made formative assessments. We all made our own, and looking back now, I wonder how aligned they were to the written curriculum standards.

Today is a different story altogether. As a state, we have yearly high-stakes, aligned state assessments that provide information about the achievement of each student. Most districts provide common interim assessments and/or pre-and post-unit assessments for each of the core academic subject areas. This is on top of the more informal and formative assessments that teachers still make and use on a regular basis to gauge student understanding. In essence, with the abundance of data now available, it is possible to accurately pinpoint areas of student need in order to provide appropriate intervention. The blessing of abundant data, however, has turned into a curse for many—and understandably so.

Recently, one principal revealed the frustration her teams were facing in managing data. Each team's achievement meeting began with the principal sharing much of the available data on each student. It was organized in a spreadsheet with student names in list format on the left and each of the assessment data points in columns across the top. There must have been at least 15 columns of data for each student. During the hour-long meeting, teachers on the team went down that list and discussed students they were worried about. They talked about negative behaviors as well as low scores on particular state and local assessments that concerned them. And at the end of the scheduled meeting time they hadn't even gotten through all the students that needed attention. There was a palpable sense of anguish in the room as the teachers left. They had spent the hour scratching the surface of the issues plaguing their students, overwhelmed by the information and unsure of what to do with it.

Although the above two situations are opposites, the outcome of each was the same—classroom instruction did not change.

The Indecisive School Improvement Team

At one school, the school improvement team consisted of a teacher representative from each grade-level team, along with the reading specialist, the guidance counselor, and the administration. Other teachers would attend certain school improvement team meetings if the topic to be discussed interested them. And that is exactly what happened at meetings—discussion. The School Improvement Team (SIT) discussed behavior programs for the cafeteria, arrival and dismissal procedures, recess schedules, and other administrative issues. As is the case in many schools, there was little discussion about any-thing that happened in classrooms, between teachers and students. Mike Schmoker (2006) would describe this situation as an example of the "buffer": "a protective barrier that discourages and even punishes close, constructive scrutiny of instruction and the supervision of instruction" (p. 13). The buffer kept the peace at these SIT meetings because no topic of real consequence was ever broached. No critical discussion of data and instructional practice took place.

> The buffer operates at several levels and with devastating conse-quences: it prevents teachers from knowing what or how well they or their colleagues teach. It deprives them of any meaningful frame of reference and discourages them from learning from each other. (Schmoker, 2006, p. 14)

At these meetings, data was shared but not analyzed for root cause. Mem-bers were frustrated. They wanted to make decisions that mattered, act upon information and measure the results. Moreover, they yearned for commit-ment from the team—a stable group of people who were dedicated to meet-ing regularly and solving problems together. They had been hurt by a few staff members who would attend meetings sporadically, only when the topic personally interested them. Then these staff members would use the meeting time to lobby the group regarding that specific issue, only to never show up again. These negative experiences were sometimes enough to stunt progress toward change. Finally, many team representatives were not instructional team leaders/department chairs. So, similar to the SIT described in Chapter 1, they didn't feel comfortable making decisions, albeit non-instructional, for their teams. They feared being judged by their colleagues. Therefore, when decisions needed to be made in SIT, the representatives went back to their teams and tried to reach consensus. Then the team decision was brought back to the SIT for more discussion. Since the SIT met only once or twice per month, it could take months to make and act upon one decision. The team itself had no authority to make decisions. In essence, it was impotent to effect change.

The School Improvement Dissertation

Each summer, a similar tradition occurs at virtually every school in the nation—the obligatory writing of the school improvement plan. And while the effort begins at the right place, analyzing available data, the process can go off the tracks pretty quickly thereafter.

Most districts provide schools with a framework to use when devising their improvement plans, complete with particular indicators that all schools must address. These indicators can run the gamut from increasing parent participation, student attendance, and cultural proficiency to decreasing disruptive behavior. In his groundbreaking book *Results*, Schmoker (2001) reminds us that schools' goals are often unrelated to student achievement (p. 1). I don't think anyone would disagree that all of the above concerns are important, even vital, to a successful school, but when they are all to be addressed simultaneously, while also addressing student achievement, the task becomes unrealistic. If you focus on everything, you will end up focusing on nothing.

When I began as an assistant principal, the SIT plan was a bound, 23-page document that described a myriad of goals to attain with many strategic actions to be taken. It was obvious that many hours of hard work and care had gone into preparing it. The plan was impressive—and the plan was overwhelming.

> Perhaps the most pervasive myth in change leadership is that planning—particularly complex, large-scale, and supposedly "strategic" planning—leads to effective change . . . the evidence for that proposition is absent not only in education but in the business world as well . . . schools that excelled in format had lower achievement. (Reeves, 2009, p. 42–43)

The downside to this written plan was that many of the goals were unrelated to student achievement and most of the strategic actions were global in nature, unable to speak to specific instructional changes that would be made on a daily basis. It wasn't easy to implement. But most importantly, this plan lived on the shelf in the principal's office. Most teachers had never even seen this document, ensuring that no real change would occur.

Looking back, I think the plan was written mainly with compliance in mind, for it addressed all of the district goals at the time. It also included the priorities of particular stakeholder groups, who each regularly exert pressure on school leaders. To decide not to include their individual interests would have been to invite judgment.

> One of the greatest dangers to a successful improvement effort is losing focus, which results from trying to take on more than we have time and resources to realistically achieve. . . . Among the hardest decisions a school community must make is to decide democratically which goals reflect the school's highest priorities—and which it must pursue later. (Schmoker, 2000, p. 33)

The bottom line is that when improvement planning gets complicated, when there are too many competing priorities, nothing changes at the classroom level. Overcoming the fear of stakeholder judgment is essential to setting the right priorities.

Why Do We Allow Ourselves to Take No Action?

 Need for Mastery vs. Fear of Failure

Whether it's due to an overabundance of data, a monstrosity of an improvement plan, or an inability to prioritize, in the end, we aren't changing what we do in front of students every day. This ensures that the level of student achievement remains unchanged. If students aren't meeting standards, then continuing the status quo means failure for our students and, therefore, our schools. So why don't we take action when doing nothing ensures failure?

School leaders don't because it's less risky to the emotions. It is especially risky for principals who taught before the accountability movement and never got the opportunity to develop their own sense of efficacy. They may not believe that they would have been able to get the results that are expected today. And if they don't believe in themselves, it may be difficult to believe in their teachers. These leaders may even feel guilty asking something of their teachers that they believe is unrealistic, if not impossible.

To lead others in change takes risk tolerance. Think about how many people you know who live very safe lives in very safe neighborhoods and go to work in very safe jobs—avoiding all risks and opportunities. I know quite a few, including myself sometimes. Let's face it: what drove some into the field of education was the need for safety and security. A school leader who analyzes data, sets an academic area of priority, identifies new instructional

Opportunity for Reflection

What situations have caused you/your school to take no action to improve learning?

Describe a time when the fear of failure kept your teachers from trying something new.

How did you, as the school leader, react?

practices, and helps teachers implement and monitor them stands alone on a stage for all to see. To try and fail hurts more than to never try at all.

The Antidote: Develop the Courage to Take Needed Action

Set Your Intention

In order to push past the fear of failure, school leaders must accept the risk that they might not get the outcome they want. In this acceptance comes the freedom to strive for an authentic sense of worth. While the fear of failure causes inaction, its counterpart, the need for mastery, goads us to try something new—to believe in ourselves. It inspires the hope that we can become more effective leaders than we've ever imagined.

Therefore, deliberately set your intention to find an authentic sense of worth by leading a school that boldly tries new things (and old things) and gets breakthrough results. I promise you that you don't need a school of superstar teachers or an unlimited budget to start increasing achievement tomorrow. All you need is a core of competent teachers and the will to live out your intention.

It's like getting mentally prepared to run a marathon. You wouldn't get up one morning and enter a race without having trained for it. The body's capacity needs to be slowly developed over time and the mind must be trained to overcome the brain's signals screaming for it to stop the discomfort. Over time, the mind gets prepared for the pain it will register and develops the will to push through it in order to accomplish the goal. The same can be said for taking action to improve achievement. You can't take action to fix everything simultaneously. Prioritize, start slowly, and train the mind to endure. It is wise to start on the global level of the School Improvement Team and foster the courage of your leaders while you grow your own.

To begin, commit to requiring a one-page improvement plan for each team based on the most worrisome vital sign from your data (see Figure 4.1). This page should list one academic goal—two at most—with a section to identify the root cause of the underlying student weakness. In this way, teachers are guided to take collective ownership as a faculty of the deficits they find. It should also include one or two new instructional practices that all teachers on the given team will implement to achieve the stated goal, along with built-in intervals to measure progress toward the goal. Checking in at agreed-upon times throughout the school year will allow you to make changes to

FIGURE 4.1 School Improvement Plan

School Year _____   Team _____

Team Members _____

Goal (What will our students be able to do?)

Root Cause (What specific competency has held them back?)

New Instructional Practices (What will we do to address the eficit area?)

Implementation (Who will implement the practices and how often?)

Evidence (How will we measure growth toward our goal?)

Timeline (How often will we measure growth?)

instructional strategies as necessary. This plan may not look substantially different than what you're used to filling out each summer. But the contrast is not in the components of the plan so as much as it is in the focus and simplicity of the plan. If you take this template and fill it with five goals and ten new instructional strategies, you've fallen into the old trap once again. One page. That's all you get and that's all it takes. Each teacher should be able to quickly skim one sheet to review the components of what they are to do to improve learning. If you work in a district that demands a dissertation for an improvement plan, comply. Turn in your bound beauty, just don't show it to your staff.

Build Trust

Since the fear at work here is fear of failure, it is important for school leaders to build a safety net for teachers. The following components make up a safety net that helps build trust between administrators and teachers.

Collaborative Data Analysis and Decision Making

Many teachers may question their own ability to analyze data, set priorities, and choose appropriate interventions and strategies, especially at first. By working through these processes collaboratively, ideas will be considered more thoroughly, and problem-solving processes will be modeled for staff.

Collective Responsibility

When decisions are made collaboratively, everyone is in the school improvement process together. When an idea turns out to be wildly successful, everyone is successful. And when an idea turns out to be ineffective or even disastrous, everyone fails together. In this way, no one has to face failing alone. In the case of collective failure, it is the responsibility of the principal, without skipping a beat, to say, "Okay. We tried this and it didn't work. Let's figure out why and decide on what we're going to try next to address the problem." This strategy lessens the pain and duration of feelings of failure, and focuses everyone's attention on the future. It also drives the point home that failure is a normal prerequisite to success.

I still remember the first day of my intermediate student teaching placement. I was so nervous, so afraid of doing something wrong and being deemed "not teacher material." To make matters worse, I had been assigned to a fifth-grade class filled with students who had behavior and learning difficulties. I had endured four years of putting myself through college to get to this point. The stakes were high. I needed to succeed. So as I packed up to go home on that first day, I confessed to my cooperating teacher that I was apprehensive, unsure of my abilities. She turned and stated frankly, "Oh, you *will* be successful." At first I didn't know if this was a threat or a promise. But as the days passed, I began to understand the level of support and collaboration that she was prepared to provide. Her safety net gave me the confidence I needed to meet that challenge. My success was to be her success.

Campaign: Identify the Pain and the Gain

Now that you've set your intention and built trust with teachers, it's time to campaign. By this, I mean taking the opportunity to sell your new idea to your staff. In this case, we will look at how to get your teachers excited about taking action—changing their daily instructional practices in order to improve student achievement.

When influencing a teacher to make change, it is imperative to speak to the old brain first. This brain will detect signs of change and switch into a defensive mode, striving to ensure safety and security. Remember that, much of the time, teachers are driven by the same fears as their leaders. And in this case, just as their principals, teachers are impacted by the fear of failure. Comfortable in the way they currently instruct—and perhaps unable to see the connection between their instruction and their results—many teachers would prefer to continue old habits. The fear of change may trigger the fight-or-flight response. Teachers experiencing these reactions may be outwardly hostile, verbally tearing down new ideas; or they may avoid learning opportunities, preserving at least their own status quo.

In speaking to the old brain, skilled school leaders will quickly identify the **pain** that teachers currently experience when they take no action to improve learning. Then the principal must show how teachers and their students will **gain** or benefit from changing instruction.

Schools that don't take action to improve student learning generally have low to mediocre achievement results. This weighs on the emotions of teachers within the building. Most of the teachers I've met and worked with over the years want to do well. They yearn to be respected by administrators, peers, and the community. This **need for respect** is more than enough fodder to stoke the desire for change and increase teachers' risk tolerance. When teachers are unable to show increased student learning, it causes emotional pain, whether or not teachers are willing to speak about it. Therefore, the pain that teachers currently face is the **fear of judgment**.

During my first months as an administrator, numerous teachers told me in confidence that they wanted our school to be respected. They wanted to be seen as putting students first, doing whatever it took to make them successful. They desired being invited to participate in curriculum projects, to lead staff development sessions, and to model successful practices. They wanted to be esteemed by fellow educators in the district and state.

It is up to the school leader to address this **pain** by communicating that you understand how they're feeling. The school may not be getting kudos from others because achievement hasn't been what they'd like it to be. Recognize that many teachers could be both overwhelmed and disillusioned by some of the improvement practices that have been implemented over the years. Each year, there's been a new focus, not necessarily academic in nature. And just before teachers have felt comfortable with one practice, it is abandoned in favor of another. Acknowledge that they have been working very hard, yet the efforts haven't yielded the wanted results. You know it doesn't feel good. So we're going to do something about it. We're going to work together on the basics of aligned instruction. And then we'll introduce new strategies until we find what works for us and gets the results we're looking for.

Finally, address the **gain** or benefit that taking action will provide. Explain that student achievement will rise, and quickly. Students will be successful and the community will take notice. This is one of the most powerful motivators I've ever come across.

Show Clear Contrast

Remember, the old brain isn't the seat of intellectual reasoning. Instead, it takes in sensory input—especially visual—and makes rapid decisions. Appeal to the old brain by showing teachers how your plan is different and better than what they've been doing in the most concise way possible. It might be communicated by holding up the SIT plan and explaining that it is unrealistic. It's too much for anyone to focus on and has too many actions that already busy teachers are supposed to implement simultaneously. Acknowledge that students have suffered because of it.

Opportunity for Reflection

How can taking action and seeing results for students provide an authentic sense of worth? For you? For your teachers?

What might happen if you were to skip the step of **identifying the pain and the gain** for teachers?

Then hold up one sheet of paper and make it clear that things will be different from now on. We will set priorities and come up with a plan together that fits on this page. It will be reasonable, everyone will feel confident in implementing it, and it will get us the results we want. We're going to stop talking about what we're going to do, and we're going to do something. The result will be unprecedented gains in student learning.

Build Expertise Together

Start the process by building the expertise of your teacher leaders in a safe, fear-free environment. Successfully changing instruction at the broadest level (the school level) takes place predominately through the vehicle of the School Improvement Team. The following ideas empower teacher leaders on the SIT to influence what goes on behind the classroom doors of their schools.

Highly Structure the School Improvement Process

Rule 1: Instructional Team Leaders are SIT members. The team's chances of being effective rest in its ability to effect change. In order to effect change, team members must be able to influence the instructional practices of teachers within the school. In most cases, a team's instructional leader or department chair has much more of a chance to influence team members than does a random teacher from the team. Still, many SITs try to function without these important leaders, impotent to cause change. When I come across a team like this, I usually ask why the team leaders are not members of the school improvement team. The answer is always that team leaders chose not to be, feeling it was too much work. If team leaders feel this way, they lack an understanding of what the team leadership entails. If they had a clear understanding of the powerful influencers they could *and should be* in their schools, they would never give up membership on the team that would teach them how to do so. Administrators may not recognize this truth either. In allowing the team leader to defer his or her SIT position to someone else, administrators feel as though they are spreading the workload more equitably. In reality, this one kind gesture disables the entire improvement team.

Rule 2: SIT membership is stable. I've never come across a school improvement team with the problem of too many dedicated members. (I'm sure one exists somewhere.) In most cases, not even team leaders wish to be on the team because it is seen as a commitment that will generate more work for its members. Moreover, most SITs operate in an open manner, allowing interested staff to attend whenever it strikes their fancy. So why join? When interest in becoming a member of the School Improvement Team is low, the administration must generate real, palpable reasons for joining the team.

To increase awareness throughout the school that the team is legitimate and working diligently to improve student learning, close membership. Besides yourself and assistant principals, allow only team leaders, a small number of others seen as crucial leaders in the building, and a parent representative. This group will remain stable over the course of the school year, allowing trust to develop between members and work to be done efficiently. In this environment, teachers will feel safe to learn together, discuss problems, and resolve real issues. Fear will be kept under control. Once a quarter, an improvement team representative will share what the team has accomplished with the staff at a faculty meeting.

Keeping membership in the team based on those who are committed, active leaders in the school will also generate interest and esteem. We all recognize that restricting access increases interest. This is what made Studio 54 the most sought-out nightclub in the country during the 1970s. Its owners understood the power of exclusivity on the human psyche and used it to their advantage. But do we want the school improvement process to be exclusive, leaving out many who may want to join? Absolutely not! However, when no one is interested in joining, it is the place to start. After the SIT is established and respected for its work, then membership should be reopened with the caveat that joining the team is a year-long commitment.

Rule 3: Give the School Improvement Team legitimate authority. Another reason for poor participation in the School Improvement Team is the belief that the administration will make the important decisions of the school anyway. This is why it is imperative to make important decisions as a SIT and then support the members as they go out into the school to implement them. Every staff member must be made aware of the new expectations and responsibilities of SIT members, so staff may understand the reasons behind new demands of their team leaders. Once team leaders realize the decision-making authority they have gained through functioning as SIT members, they will be reluctant to give it up. Through collaboration with other team leaders and administrators, they will set academic goals for their team, decide on strategic actions that will be taken by their team, and determine formative assessment measures to monitor their team's progress. And as other school staff sees this change, they will become more interested in participating in school leadership opportunities.

Rule 4: Keep student achievement the focus of the School Improvement Team. Time is one of the most valuable commodities in the business of education. So the time set aside for school improvement must be used to deal only with the issue of increasing student achievement. This rule will prevent the group from being sidetracked with issues that have no bearing on student progress. Other, more managerial issues can be addressed in a separate meeting of instructional team leaders only.

Rule 5: Write a short, focused school improvement plan. One winter, my husband became ill in the middle of the night. I called 911 and we were at the hospital in a flash. When the paramedics rolled him into the back of the emergency room, the waiting resident ran toward us and asked, "What are his vitals?" The paramedics quickly shared the data they had gathered on the ride to the hospital, allowing the doctors to decide on a plan and take action. All of this happened in about two minutes.

Let me reiterate what information the resident asked for. He was interested in his heart rate, his blood pressure, his blood oxygen concentration, and whether or not he was breathing. He did not ask about the mole on his back (which I've been calling suspicious for years), nor did he want to know about the headaches he sometimes gets right before it rains. This information would have only complicated the situation, delaying life-saving action. We must start using this medical model when considering school improvement if we are to create actionable plans.

Help your teacher leaders identify major areas of need for the school and for their teams using summative data. This big picture activity will help to familiarize them with the process of looking at data together as a school improvement team, and setting priorities. At this point, other forms of collected data should be consulted in order to triangulate the areas of most weakness. Finding at least three different pieces of data that point to the same weakness lends credence to the assumption that a true problem has been identified. Next, collaborate to help each team leader set a reasonable goal to improve the prioritized area of weakness. While I've witnessed increases of 30 percentage points in a single year, a five percent increase from the prior year is very reasonable. When creating the goal, write it in a way that is easy to understand and measure. For example: 96% of third graders will score proficient or advanced in the area of general reading on the state assessment.

Then, help team leaders determine how they will measure progress toward this goal throughout the school year (more on this in Chapter 5). Be sure that dates to check progress are agreed upon. Finally, the entire SIT should collaborate to help team leaders choose the instructional strategic actions they will use as a grade-level team to increase achievement. At the end of the SIT plan writing session, each team should have a one page plan that simply states what its goal/goals are and why, what each teacher will do to ensure the goal is met, and how progress will be monitored through the year. A section to identify the root cause of the deficit area is included to ensure that teachers make the connection between school practice and results (see Figure 4.1, page 51). This simple plan should be kept in the front of each teacher's plan book and referred to often. It must then be revised throughout the course of the year as certain strategic actions found to be ineffective are replaced by new strategic actions. Using a concise plan such as this will keep student learning experiences aligned to the team's goal, and help avoid misaligned activities.

As a part of a district process, an administrator visited a secondary school that was having difficulty meeting state proficiency standards in the area of reading. Before arriving, she had expected to see and hear about the interventions that the leadership team had put into place to address specific deficiencies in reading instruction. What she found was a school of great teachers hard at work—implementing new practices in order to be awarded "Green School" status. Teacher leaders, with the help of central office staff, were conducting professional development sessions in order to train teachers in the implementation of the new eco-friendly lessons, practices, and paperwork. However, there were no extra efforts devoted to addressing the dire issue of students unable to read and comprehend at grade level. Metaphorically, the students' hearts had stopped beating and instead of administering CPR, the staff was busy screening for a possible thyroid problem.

In our schools, there are innumerable opportunities for enriching our students' education. But we face limited time and limited resources, and attempting to focus on everything means that needed action will be delayed or stopped all together. We must prioritize students' vital signs and take action that will impact core academic achievement.

Rule 6: Hold the team accountable for increased academic achievement. In many schools, School Improvement Teams come together in the late summer to write their improvement plan. Then they get together periodically through the school year to discuss issues. And that's all that happens. As data comes in throughout the school year, they fail to analyze it to determine the effectiveness of their decisions. When the standardized test results arrive in the early summer, rarely do they go back to see if the goals they set were met. In order for the SIT to be effective, they must experience accountability to balance their authority—accountability to each other, to staff, to students, and to the community. They must understand that increased student achievement rests largely in their hands—in their ability to influence the instructional practices of their teammates. They must have a sense of urgency about getting that job done.

Opportunity for Reflection

What would happen if you were to implement the SIT rules without first building trust?

Which of the rules are already in place in your school? Which rule would have the biggest positive impact on your school? Why?

During my time as an administrator, the SIT was required to present the SIT plan to the faculty and staff at the beginning of every year. This entailed each team leader describing his team's goals, actions, and assessment measures. Then, at the end of the school year, we held a "State of the School" meeting in which team leaders led their teams in sharing with faculty and staff whether or not their goals were met. This meeting always took on a celebratory tone (complete with faux champagne), even when all teams didn't quite meet their goals. Those teams shared how close they came, lessons they learned, and what they were planning to do differently in the following year. This practice is an example of "transparency" described by Fullan (2008) as one of the six secrets of change:

> When data are precise, presented in a nonjudgmental way, considered by peers, and used for improvement as well as for external accountability, they serve to balance pressure and support. . . . Transparency involves being open about the results and practices and is essentially an exercise in pursuing and nailing down problems that recur and identifying evidence-informed responses to them. (p. 98–99)

It was a truly a special time that everyone looked forward to. Teams took pride in a year of hard work together, and in the tangible results it garnered. It was the reward for their risks.

5

Fearless Decision: Acknowledging Standardized Test Results

All professions have indicators of success. Following are some familiar examples:

- ♦ **Lawyers:** how many cases they win
- ♦ **Doctors:** how many patients they make well
- ♦ **Tax Accountants:** how much money they save their clients
- ♦ **Financial Advisors:** how much money they make for their clients through investments
- ♦ **Business Owners/CEOs:** how much profit they make through the sale of goods or services

Their success or failure is seen clearly through market demand. These professionals either flourish or fail based on their ability to gain and retain clients or customers. This reality demands continuous improvements and innovations in order to stay competitive and increase market share.

Conversely, in the field of education, there are few indicators of success to assure stakeholders of our competence. Moreover, the public indicators that do exist—primarily standardized assessments—have been devalued, even shunned by the educational community. Nancy Ichinaga, principal of Bennett Elementary, states, "Every profession uses objective measures to determine effectiveness. Educators don't like the results of their tests, so they condemn the measure. But only a poor workman quarrels with his tools" (Carter, 2001, p. 25). Mike Schmoker (2000) states that "schools have an almost cultural and ingrained aversion to reckoning with, much less living by, results" (p. 3). He goes on to explain that "a deep and debilitating confusion about how means relate to ends has always been one of the marks of the teaching profession" (p. 3). This seeming avoidance of accountability has led to the mistrust of public schooling by society at large, especially since public educators have historically enjoyed a captive clientele. Unlike the professions listed above, our customers have not enjoyed the luxury of choice.

It is imperative here to put high-stakes testing into perspective, acknowledging both the intended and unintended consequences of and problems with their implementation. In some states, the state assessment and the curriculum in the various districts are out of alignment. And while they give us valuable information, one consequence of high-stakes assessment is teachers failing to teach all core curriculums (social studies and science), so that more and more time can be spent in the tested areas of reading and mathematics. The key is to teach reading and math effectively within the time allotted, rather than teaching it ineffectively all day long.

Remember that standardized assessments are but one piece of important data to which every school has access. These results should be regarded along with local and school assessments to gain a more complete view of student achievement and to plan strategically. Problems only arise when this information is either viewed as an exclusive indicator of school success or when it is ignored by school leaders and teachers, breaking the connection between actions and results—the problem we will examine here.

Let's take a look at some of the most common reasons for disregarding standardized assessment results given by school leaders:

1. State assessments are void of rigor.
2. State assessments fail to measure what is important to teach in schools.
3. It is unfair to expect our lower performing students to pass state assessments.

Although reasons 1 and 3 seem to be in conflict, quite often they are given by the same school leader and many times all three beliefs are held. In the next session, each reason will be explored on a deeper level in order to understand its basis in fear. The remainder of the chapter will focus on solutions.

Reason 1: State or High-Stakes Assessments Are Void of Rigor

Each year, I spend some time examining the public release items for the state high-stakes assessments. And every time I engage in this process, a number of test questions surface that surprise me by their high level of rigor. These items tend to require students to use higher-level thinking skills such as analyzing and evaluating. Students must make inferences, draw conclusions, and possess adequate content knowledge in order to show proficiency. In fact, if I had to complete these exercises, I would need to go back into the selection, reread, and contemplate before answering the selected response question or constructing a written response. But because all questions directly align with an assessed objective in the state curriculum, which span the rigor continuum, not all questions are as challenging. And due to the limitations of the format, there aren't opportunities for students to be involved in authentic real-world, interdisciplinary problem-solving. Therefore, the state assessment with which I am most familiar includes a level of rigor that some state assessments may not, while still having some shortcomings.

So, if it may be true that some standardized tests are *not* rigorous enough, why shouldn't the results be ignored? Because they still provide useful information to all stakeholders about the strengths and weaknesses of a school's instructional program. And our students have the right to master the content and skills identified for mastery at their grade level. Only schools achieving at 100% in all tested areas have the right to disregard the results to focus on other competencies.

One principal reported that her staff, who thought the high-stakes assessment was not a valid measure of achievement—and had spent their time and energy in other areas—changed after viewing the results. The data showed that the two nearest middle schools had 10% higher levels of student proficiency in reading. They had the lowest reading scores in their region. In one year, this principal's school results increased by 10% with no systemic overhaul to instructional practices. Each teacher's attitude had been transformed, refocusing them on the written curriculum and influencing their daily actions.

The point is if you believe that your state's assessment is void of rigor, then ethically you must raise the challenge level for the students in your school. But this can be accomplished while keeping instruction aligned to state and local curriculum standards. Your students will benefit from increased expectations and will still be able to master the concepts included in the high-stakes assessment. For instance, if your teachers spend instructional time teaching students to evaluate author's craft (which is a higher-level skill), your students will still be able to comprehend grade-level text (a lower-level skill) and do well on the assessment. If in mathematics, your teachers spend more time on reasoning and representation, your students will still be able to complete simple multiplication problems. Much of this argument should be put to rest with the adoption of common core standards and their assessments, which are predicted to be more rigorous than many current state tests and more in line with National Assessment of Educational Progress (NAEP) expectations.

The problem is many of the school leaders who worry about the lack of rigor in the assessments are the same ones who struggle to help their students pass. Our students need basic competencies in order to engage in complex ideas and issues. E. D. Hirsch (1996), founder and chairman of the Core Knowledge Foundation and professor emeritus of education and humanities at the University of Virginia, writes, "There are no real-world examples of adults with information-age competencies who are functioning with a fourth-grade vocabulary" (p. 145). We must now work to identify the true nature of the issue here. Why do some school leaders disregard standardized assessment data?

Need for Mastery vs. Fear of Failure

It's like the guy who comes home from a job interview, excited about the prospect of a new opportunity, only to disparage the position once he discovers that the company selected another applicant. Or like the child who, after losing at checkers, upturns the board and leaves the room, refusing to continue participation in the game. It's human nature. When we believe we cannot succeed at something, we avoid it. When we can't avoid it, we belittle and criticize it to keep it from hurting us.

One new secondary school principal described his staff as aloof to standardized assessments. For years before he arrived, they had been using portfolios to evaluate student learning and felt that this form of assessment was "right," garnering information regarding the higher-level abilities of students, as opposed to the "wrong" approach of traditional selected response tests. After many conversations between the principal and the teachers over a period of time, the staff began to understand the value of preparing students to show what they know in many different formats. But soon after reaching that conclusion, fear bubbled to the service with questions like:

♦ What percentage of our student population has to pass?
♦ What will happen to teachers whose students don't pass?
♦ How will we fit in all the stuff that's tested that we haven't been teaching?

These questions uncovered the teachers' fears of professional failure as well as alignment issues between assessment, written curriculum, and taught curriculum. We'll take a closer look at how this principal moved his staff past their fears later in the chapter.

Reason 2: State Assessments Fail to Measure What Is Important to Teach in Schools

This reason for disregarding standardized test data is grounded in the identity crisis that has held public schools in its grip for decades. Who are we and what are we here to do? As a profession, we cannot seem to agree on the answers to these questions, nor are we willing to take up the cause and flesh it out. Instead, every school in the country creates separate mission, vision, and belief statements that may or may not be aligned with one another and that take students in different directions. A quick, online jaunt turned up these listed below:

- ◆ "To provide each student a diverse education in a safe, supportive environment that promotes self-discipline, motivation, and excellence in learning . . . to assist the students in developing skills to become independent and self-sufficient adults who will succeed and contribute responsibly in a global community" (Marion School District 2).
- ◆ "To guide its students to be critically thinking, informed and empowered agents of positive change in their communities" (Social Justice Academy, Ulysses S. Grant High School).
- ◆ "To develop a community of learners in which all students acquire the knowledge, skills, and confidence to meet the challenges of a changing and increasingly diverse society" (Franklin Elementary School).
- ◆ "To provide a nurturing environment where all members are important" (Commonwealth Elementary).
- ◆ "To develop students' higher-level thinking skills, problem-solving and coping behaviors; to help students define their values and goals; and, to cause students to respect themselves and the rights of others" (Academy Elementary).
- ◆ "To ensure that each child will be challenged to think critically, to problem solve" (Crockett Elementary).

School leaders' intentions for their students run the gamut from helping them develop high self-esteem to encouraging them to become social activists. Many school leaders do not view high academic achievement as the primary outcome for students who spend time in their schools. In fact, one study of 108 elementary schools' mission statements found that only 59 focused on academic success. But what was telling was that of the 59 who *did* focus on academic success, most—almost double—were deemed successful in student achievement based on standardized assessment data (Craft, Slate, & Bustamante, 2009). As was discovered in a 2008 research study by Slate, Jones, Wiesman, Alexander, and Saenz, the mission statements of high-performing schools had an explicit focus on academic success (Craft et al.). Academically successful schools know that high student achievement is their job. Therefore, they embrace assessment data as confirmation that their carefully planned actions have garnered results. So why do so many school leaders downplay standardized assessment data in an effort to focus on outcomes other than student achievement?

 ## Need for a Sense of Meaning and Purpose vs. Fear of Purposelessness

School leaders want the best for their students and for society. In deciding to become leaders, they've made a commitment to something bigger than themselves; they usually hold higher concerns. They hope their graduates can go off and lead happy, fulfilled lives—while making the world a better place. Today, we find ourselves as global citizens, sometimes feeling as though we are watching our world hurtle toward destruction through the results of climate change, natural disasters, wars over oil and religion, etc. Our students will need to be part of the solution. Where we can't agree as professionals is how to attain this result.

Many principals feel that focusing on academic achievement lacks purpose in light of more pressing demands. Therefore, we see leaders strive to feel purposeful by influencing student values, beliefs, and goals. The problem is that without high levels of academic competence, our students will be left behind in the intellectual global marketplace, unable to procure the jobs necessary for them to make a difference. Already, U.S. students trail others in multiple measures of academic achievement.

Reason 3: It Is Unfair to Expect Our Lower Performing Students to Pass State Assessments

This reason, that it is unfair, seems to take the side of the child, to protect him from the unrealistic expectations and compliance pressures of a system that will, in the end, cause him to develop low self-esteem. No one wants to set up a child for failure. Yet the only way a student will experience failure is if we as school leaders allow it. My belief is that any student working for a traditional high school diploma should be proficient in the knowledge and skills necessary to pass standardized assessments. I do believe that there are students in our schools who, due to impaired cognitive ability, will not be able to meet minimum diploma standards and therefore should be offered an alternative diploma track. The problem rests with students who have normal aptitude, but who aren't performing up to grade-level standards. Far too often we conclude that because they aren't making it, they *cannot* make it. We give up and call the minimum expectations unfair.

Yes, many school leaders hold this belief, though unwilling to admit it. But, we have to look below the surface here to find the fear hiding beneath. The real belief at work here is that it is unfair to ask educators to do the nearly impossible—bring all students up to at least grade-level standards.

When Sharon Brittingham was the principal of Frankford Elementary, she experienced this sentiment from her staff.

> At the time, she said the attitude of the teaching staff was . . . that teachers couldn't be expected to produce academic achievement with so little to work with, demographically speaking. "We had some battles," Brittingham said. She told the teachers, "If you don't believe all children can learn, what are you here for?" (Chenoweth, 2008, p. 19)

 ## Need for Mastery vs. Fear of Failure

The influences on student achievement that are beyond our control are vast—poverty, divorce, abuse, neglect, and mental health issues, just to name some. It is enough to make any school leader feel they are fighting an uphill battle. But to feel it is impossible or just too difficult for struggling students to meet proficiency standards uncovers a deep fear of failure. It is much safer to the ego to disregard achievement data.

Antidote: Develop the Courage to Acknowledge Standardized Assessment Data

Set Your Intention

What is your emotional relationship with data? When people talk data, how do you feel? Many can feel the anxiety set in at the mention of it. If you are in this situation, begin by viewing data as neutral information—kind of like the sort of data that the gauges on your dashboard provide. Mentally frame your school's data as a diagnostic check up. You probably don't get nervous when your gas gauge starts to point to Empty. Instead, you see it as a call to action. You go fill the tank.

Achievement data can feel the same way if you allow it. It points to a specific area that needs attention. And if you respond with an appropriate intervention, the problem is resolved.

This doesn't mean that you'll never feel negative feelings around data. You may experience disappointment or fear due to certain results, which is normal. Develop courage by intending to use the information constructively, even in the midst of these emotions. Setting a new intention here requires a change of heart and mind. Sheri Shirley and the staff at Oakland Heights Elementary had a "willingness to change and look at difficult facts without flinching. Shirley said she has embraced those feelings of discomfort that change represents, and she expects her teachers to, as well" (Chenoweth, 2008, p. 45). She added that if her scores dip, they'll just pull out the state standards again and reexamine them (p. 45).

If you have negative feelings surrounding the role of high-stakes assessment, take some time to examine the thoughts behind them. Whether they are the fear-based reasons discussed in the beginning of the chapter or just a general sense of resentment over being put upon by outside forces, begin to move out of that defensive emotional posture.

Try to approach the situation from another perspective—perhaps from the point-of-view of a parent. How would you feel if your own child attended a school that didn't fare well on standardized assessments and didn't seem to mind? Our stakeholders in the community both need and deserve proof of stewardship with public funds and with the children they entrust to us. To regain and keep trust we can at least show competence on public measures of success and a transparency in the improvement process. In order to earn an authentic sense of professional worth, commit to high academic achievement for your students. While it shouldn't be our end goal to achieve superior high-stakes assessment results, if we are doing the right thing for students day in and day out, they will easily be able to reach proficiency on knowledge and skills we are contracted to teach. Moreover, the ability to demonstrate understanding on multiple types of assessments will open doors of opportunity for students in preparation for university learning, trade school/vocational learning, or the work force. Paying appropriate attention to standardized assessment data is a positive step toward taking responsibility and developing efficacy as a school.

Build Trust

As well as the general building trust suggestions in Chapter 2, the following actions will help move your staff toward strategic use and appreciation of standardized assessment data. Since much of teacher resistance will be rooted in fear of failure and fear of purposelessness, the actions utilized must first mitigate these anxieties.

To Mitigate Fear of Failure: Begin by Building the Capacity of Your Instructional Leaders

During SIT meeting time, or another time carved out for instructional leaders/department chairs to meet, start to discuss their feelings around standardized assessment. Taking the temperature of this group will provide guidance in how to proceed. (Are they stating that the assessment is too rigorous or not rigorous enough?) The goal is to build the comfort and confidence of your leaders so they may be the ones to lead their teams in the work ahead. When the time is right, they can jointly lead a faculty meeting to begin the standardized test conversation with the staff. They will also be able to lead conversations with their individual teams. If your instructional leaders are trusted members of the faculty and they believe that standardized assessment results are valid and important, it will be a much easier sell to the staff at large. When striving to transform hearts and minds, always begin with a smaller group of trusted and influential teacher leaders who can carry the torch of change through the school community.

To Mitigate Fear of Purposelessness: Develop an Understanding with Your Leaders Regarding the Imperative of High Student Achievement

This may require you to take a step back and collaboratively rewrite the school's mission, vision, and values so that student achievement is the focus. The federal government has become insistent that, above all else, our students should be able to achieve in core curriculum areas. With new Common Core Standards, every public school in the country will come into alignment under one curriculum/instruction umbrella with very similar high-stakes assessments. It won't be a choice. Teachers who fear purposelessness will need to be assured that classroom instruction and assessment can be aligned to federal and state requirements without having to mirror the format. Students should have the opportunity to participate in varying and creative learning experiences. Finally, speak to your commitment that classroom instruction and school assessments be rigorous. The standardized assessment can be seen as "the floor" or minimum competency for student learning. However,

I suspect that as the common core standards are adopted and new, aligned assessments are introduced, educators will be more comfortable that the rigor level is appropriate.

Campaign: Identify the Pain and the Gain

One of the first sources of **pain** to address should be that of poor public image of the school. In paying attention to and working to increase outward measures of success, the parents, teachers in other schools, and leaders at the local and state level will be satisfied with your performance. This will grant the school more autonomy in day-to-day matters—a big **gain**. Failing schools, on the other hand, face a loss of decision-making authority which can hurt climate and morale.

The second **pain** that should be addressed is the current "preparation for testing" that probably occurs in the school. Even schools that don't give much heed to the test often spend weeks engaged in feckless test preparation activities with students. This will stop immediately, producing an instant **gain**. Instead, teachers will teach the written curriculum to understanding—period.

The third **pain** to address is a future pain that will implant itself inside the minds of your teachers as soon as they foresee any changes on the horizon: increased workload. The underlying fear at play here is that school leaders will expect more time and more expertise than teachers can give—that there will be unrealistic expectations. And when teachers are unable to meet those, they will be judged harshly. This is a reality-based fear, since it happens every day in schools across the country. Instead, assure teachers that their workload does not have to increase substantially in order for learning to increase: a **gain**. By changing *how* their current time is used, teachers will be able to successfully make the needed changes in practice.

Show Clear Contrast

The contrast to show here is victim versus hero. In the past, teachers may have felt like victims of federal legislation and top-down expectations that they didn't even want to try to reach. With a new outlook, this can all change.

> [High achieving schools] embrace and use all the data they can get their hands-on. They want to know how their students are doing, and they know that classroom observation by teachers, though important, is fragmentary and doesn't allow overall patterns to be observed.

State test data, district data, classroom test data, and any formative assessment data they can get their hands-on are all eagerly studied. (Chenoweth, 2008, p. 217–8)

Explain to teachers that they don't have to feel like victims anymore. They will become heroes by embracing data and being champions of student achievement. Even if federal legislation didn't require standardized assessment, you would seek it out in order to obtain important information about how we're doing as a school. They will be able to rest assured that their students will be academically advanced and ready to take on the world, unlike schools that are still living in fear.

Build Expertise Together

Let's go back now to the secondary school principal in the beginning of the chapter. After uncovering his staff's fears, he first worked with his leadership team to analyze the alignment between the standardized assessment and the written and taught curriculum, paying close attention to levels of rigor. When these leaders were comfortable with what they had found, he had them lead several faculty meetings on the topic of high-stakes assessment. The teacher leaders took the staff through the same process they had participated in with the principal.

And as teachers explored the demands of the standardized assessment through public release tasks during these meetings, surprisingly they discovered that in many ways, it was more rigorous than the components and expectations of the portfolio evaluations in which they were so invested. Quickly, the taught curriculum came into alignment with the written curriculum and state assessment, and within two years, students were performing well on both the standardized assessment and the portfolios. The fear of failure had been replaced with the feeling of mastery.

At another school, a similar story played out. For years, state assessment data had been largely unexamined, which alleviated pressure on teachers, yet failed to provide them a sense of mastery. There was little way to connect actions with results. So as the leadership team began to analyze the demands of the standardized test through public release tasks, everyone began to see the tight connection between the content and rigor of the assessment and that of the state curriculum. The biggest ah-ha moment for them was that they had glossed over many of the state's learning objectives, failing to realize the levels of rigor built into each one. So they began to experiment with changing components of the instructional program, as well as their teacher-made

FIGURE 5.1. Alignment Framework

State Objective What will students learn and be able to do?
Formative Assessment How will I know when they've mastered the objective?
Instructional Strategy What learning experiences will result in student mastery?

assessments, to match the rigor of the objectives (see Figure 5.1). The faculty saw strong results right away.

Do the following steps first with your teacher leaders or SIT, then with grade-level teams. Pay close attention in each section to the common mistakes that schools make, causing the process to be ineffective and allowing fear and frustration to proliferate.

Analyze Standardized Assessment Data (Summative Data) First and Find the "Red Flags"

The red flags are the vital signs we discussed in Chapter 4. These are the problems that must be addressed immediately in order to stabilize the patient—or the school. These are urgent issues impacting achievement in core academic areas, across grade levels. If the school has not reached a high level of proficiency in the general population, that indicates a problem with the school-wide instructional program.

This is where many schools make a big mistake. The standardized assessment results arrive and, after finding the percentage of students who passed, school leaders and teachers immediately begin to examine how individual students fared. Time is spent to identify all the need areas of the students who didn't pass and elaborate plans are made to "fix" it during the next school year. When this is the process that occurs, the entire school misses out on "the big picture." No one has allowed teachers to see the commonalities in strengths and needs school-wide and on grade-level teams or in specific subject areas. It's like your GPS zooming in on a neighborhood map when you're not even sure what state you're in!

Another powerful visual is comparing a school's overall instructional program to a leaky boat. It's tempting to run around, trying to plug all the holes while the boat is slowly sinking. Instead, it's best to jump ship and build a better boat. Find the overall weakness and revamp the overall, daily instructional program for all students. Often times, changing one simple practice as a school, grade level, or department yields the greatest results.

At my school, mathematical communication came up as a weakness in all tested grades. Before thinking about making instructional changes for individual students, all math teachers came together and agreed upon the daily instructional strategies they would change in order to increase students' communication ability. These changes were planned long before any individual student data was analyzed and within weeks, resulted in measurable gains. Nothing dispels fear like confidence.

The following questions will help to clarify and identify the source of the problem. Once almost all students have met proficiency in core academics, the following questions can be skipped, as the school is ready to focus exclusively on action plans for individual students. As a school improvement team analyzes standardized test results, try to answer the following basic questions:

- ♦ As a school, in what core subject area are we the weakest? (Check the vitals.)
- ♦ Of that subject area, which subscale score is the weakest? For instance, if the weak core subject is mathematics, what is causing low achievement? Is it automaticity of basic facts, utilizing correct algorithms, problem-solving, communicating, etc.?
- ♦ Do the subscale scores point to the same area/s of weakness at most grade levels?

Plan to Measure the Impact of the Strategic Actions Teachers Will Choose

Set regular times throughout the school year to determine whether or not the chosen strategic actions are having a positive impact on student achievement. In order to measure the success of the strategic actions, an appropriate assessment must be utilized. In some cases, an assessment already mandated by or provided by the school district will suit the need. In other cases, teams may need to develop their own common tests. Remember to reiterate to teacher leaders and teaching staff that they are not being judged here. The effectiveness of the instructional action that was agreed upon is what's being measured. This should help to keep fear in check. The most important requirements of the formative assessment chosen here are as follows:

The formative assessment must directly measure the learning outcome being assessed at an *independent* student level. It may sound ridiculous to point out that the assessment must measure the targeted learning outcome. But a peek into most schools would uncover this as an issue. If the assessment does measure what it is intended, then check to see if the student must perform the learning outcome independently.

At one school, a team of teachers intended to increase student comprehension of informational text. When they discussed with school leaders how the results should be measured, one teacher suggested that the students read a non-fiction text in small reading groups. Then the teacher would lead a discussion of the text and finally ask comprehension questions during reading group time. Finally the teacher would record whether or not students answered the questions correctly.

One of the concerns with this assessment technique is that students would not have to perform it independently. They could listen to the discussion of the text before and while answering comprehension questions. These conversations would increase student understanding of the text, thus clouding a clear picture of independent reading comprehension ability. Because scaffolding learning is so necessary for students during the instructional process, many educators do not realize that scaffolding must be removed during assessment. I liken the situation to swimming lessons. When children begin swim lessons, instructors provide kickboards to assist them in staying afloat while learning proper kick techniques. But after a course of lessons, when it is time for the swim test, there are no kickboards to be found. They were removed gradually as students learned to stay afloat on their own. We, as educators, must always be moving toward student independence, removing scaffolding slowly throughout the school year until students can perform at grade level all on their own.

The formative assessment must be as rigorous as the stated curriculum objective and the standardized summative assessment. This takes careful analysis of the wording used in state or local curriculum objectives. Especially important are the action verbs used to describe what students should be able to do. Most likely, the verbs will run the spectrum from simple (e.g., *identify*) to complex (e.g., *analyze, evaluate*). The formative assessments used must require at least the same level of cognitive demand required in the written curriculum objective. One way to ensure this occurs is to study the way a specific curriculum objective could be tested on the state assessment, using available public release tasks. This activity can provide insight into creative ways to assess a specific objective.

During my time as a principal, the School Improvement Team was surprised time and time again when we took the time to analyze the rigor within a state objective and then thought divergently about the different ways that specific objectives could be assessed. We were clearly able to conclude that even when our instruction contained the appropriate rigor, our teacher-made assessments were very predictable and undemanding. By increasing the rigor and varying the format of our school assessments, we were able to identify weak areas to address immediately and our students were much more successful on the summative, standardized assessments. Requiring students to show what they know at an independent level and aligning the level of rigor on formative assessments are just two simple strategies that will produce results far greater than expected.

The formative assessment must be quick and easy for teachers to implement and grade. Professional educators sometimes have a tendency to make matters more complex than they ought to be. That's why much of what school leaders ask teachers to do never gets implemented in classrooms. Caution must be used to ensure that the formative assessment does not fall prey to this tendency. Remember, you are not a professional assessment company and you don't have to create products that are scientifically reliable here. Don't fall victim to the fear that you lack the expertise to do this. The purpose of the assessments is only to show whether teachers' instruction is working or not. It just isn't rocket science. These assessments should include only enough questions for the student to demonstrate a level of mastery of each tested objective. Therefore, students should be able to complete the assessment quickly and teachers should be able to grade it quickly. If the test is too long, either too many objectives are being assessed at once or there are too many questions representing each objective. If this is the case, teachers will have a difficult time grading and analyzing it in a timely manner. In many cases, teachers will grade it, but the thought of analyzing the results will be so overwhelming, it will never occur.

FIGURE 5.2. Simple Teacher Action Plan

What are we going to do differently in our instruction to address the area of need? What will it look like?
How will we provide coaching to students as they develop this new skill?
How will we know when students have mastered it? How will students know? What opportunities will they have to evaluate their own work and the work of others?

Plan a Strategic Action to Address this Specific Area of Weakness

When deciding on a strategic action, keep it simple. In my experience, the most effective actions are those that are easily understood and implemented by teachers. They usually involve time spent explicitly teaching and modeling the needed skill and then providing feedback to students as they progress toward mastery. Figure 5.2 provides a framework for this process.

Education reform consultant Mike Schmoker (2006) echoes this belief: "Teaching needn't be exceptional to have a profound effect; continuous commonsense efforts to even roughly conform to effective practice and essential standards will make a life-changing difference for students across all socioeconomic levels" (p. 9). If the SIT determines that staff development is needed in order for teachers to better understand the strategic actions that need to be implemented, then that should be the professional development focus for some time. However, don't wait to implement the actions until training has occurred. Instead, provide ongoing training while implementation is happening. Two questions to come to consensus on before implementation of strategic actions are:

- ◆ How often will teachers use or implement the actions?
- ◆ If someone walked into the classroom while the strategic actions were being implemented, what would be observed?

These questions will ensure agreement and commitment on what the actions should look like and how often they should be executed in the classroom. This information will increase teacher comfort with the plan, easing individual teacher anxiety.

After the formative assessment is implemented, the real work begins. This is the crucial time to analyze the results of the assessment in teams in order to discover whether or not the strategic actions are producing the desired results. It is imperative that teachers are given release time to have these conversations. I recommend using time that has traditionally been used for formal professional development, as well as the use of rolling substitutes, or providing student monitoring at a school or grade-wide student program. When analyzing this data in teams, it is important to take note of desirable results as well as poor results. Are the results poor in all classrooms or are some teachers getting good results? This is the time to discuss details of how the strategic actions are being carried out in classrooms. Teachers may benefit from visiting one another's classrooms to observe implementation and provide coaching.

Act on the Information

If the first three steps are followed, but this last step isn't, progress will not be made. This is the step that's most important and most often overlooked. I don't believe that teachers avoid this step because they don't want to follow through with it. From my experiences, I believe instead that teachers lose energy and focus along the way through this continuous improvement cycle, also known as the Plan, Do, Study, Act cycle.

It is important that principals and your skilled team leaders step in during this "Act" stage and facilitate the process. Time must be given to teachers to both study the results of formative assessments and then decide on the appropriate actions. Monitoring the "Act" portion of the process takes a commitment on the part of school leaders to be inside classrooms. Completing regular walk-throughs is the only way to know what's really going on daily.

Opportunity for Reflection

How has allowing the improvement process to become too complex
held your school back?

What instructional practices have you held onto in the face of question-
able results? What would it take for you to allow your teachers to
abandon that practice and try something else?

After three to six weeks, if the chosen strategic actions do not result in high
levels of student mastery or achievement, then *stop doing them*. This is sometimes where ideological issues can get in the way of progress—more on this
in Chapter 8. Some educators and school leaders value certain instructional
practices because they support a particular ideology or philosophy, rather
than because of the results they can produce. If something isn't working,
educators must be willing to stop doing it and try something else. And school
leaders must go further than just giving teachers permission to do this; they
must push them to do it and acknowledge them for taking the risk. Failing to
stop doing ineffective practices is what has created an overwhelming work
environment for teachers. We must take things off their plates instead of just
adding to them. Finding and implementing strategies that *do* produce results
will be the expectation in the fearless, action-oriented culture of the school.

6

Fearless Decision: Holding Teachers Accountable for Student Achievement

Almost 99% of all tenured teachers received 'satisfactory' evaluations over a three-year period in one American city (Meyer, 2010). Take a moment to consider this. More alarmingly, this data is comparable to many cities and districts.

So what are teachers paid to do? Is it to teach? Among other things, yes. But teaching is only where the 21st century teacher's responsibilities begin. As we explored in the last chapter, the real job of the current teacher is to ensure student learning. Federal No Child Left Behind and Race to the Top legislation have awoken previously slumbering educators across the nation to their charge. While many in the profession may not like or agree with this new reality, it is here and will change how we do business—starting with teacher accountability.

If ensuring student learning is what teachers get paid to do, then one would surmise that the teacher's evaluation (along with job retention) would be based, in large part, upon their students' achievement. In essence, the evaluations would mirror teachers' effectiveness. But this is not the case in most American school systems, a fact that is not lost on the teachers themselves. Todd Whitaker (2003) recounted that "some of the best teachers in the school—the teachers I most respected—told me confidentially that our evaluation process had limited value; some even considered it a joke" (p. 84). Findings of the multi-state research study *The Widget Effect* revealed a similar picture.

- Even though administrators and teachers admit that there are low performing teachers in their schools, all but approximately 1% are evaluated as satisfactory or higher.
- When so many teachers are evaluated as above average or excellent, it provides no means for recognizing those who are actually performing at those levels. This disincents superior performance.
- About 75% of teachers received no specific comments on how to improve their performance.
- Poor performance is all but ignored. None of the districts studied fired more than a few teachers a year for not meeting performance standards. (Weisberg, Sexton, Mulhern, & Keeling, 2009, p. 6)

The Denver Public Schools were among the schools studied, and after viewing the results of his district's teacher survey on evaluation, the Superintendent stated:

> The report makes clear what we are all too painfully aware of, that virtually every element of our structure on how we retain, recruit, reward, develop, and replace teachers is fundamentally misaligned with our goals of having a highly effective teacher in every classroom. (Meyer, 2010)

Okay. So we all agree that the evaluation system is broken. But why? Well, either we are afraid to tell bad teachers that they aren't meeting standards or we are evaluating the wrong thing.

What Are We Evaluating?

How do we evaluate teachers? Historically, most districts' evaluation tool has included indicators that relate to **the process of teaching**. Many describe successful planning and instructional behaviors, such as stating the objective of the lesson, asking higher-level questions, and actively engaging students in the lesson. Many also include professional characteristics such as completing work in a timely fashion and collaborating with various stakeholders and resource staff. Few evaluation tools include a significant number of indicators relating to student learning or student mastery of prescribed curriculum objectives. Therefore, teachers are rewarded for the daily processes they go through instead of the outcomes they are able to achieve. In these

Opportunity for Reflection

Would you consider your school process-oriented or results-oriented? Why?

How do you currently determine whether or not a teacher is effective? Is it an accurate measure of effectiveness?

process-oriented schools, the teacher who "looks like" she's doing a good job, joins every school committee, and shows a good attitude toward administrators is rated as effective or perhaps even excellent. I once worked for a principal who walked around the school on snow days to see which teachers had cheated death on the highways to be at work—for those (in her mind) were the truly dedicated. What we're missing here is that many teachers who are committed to the field and do what looks like good practice are not effective for various reasons. It would be like calling someone a great attorney because she spends so much time on research, meeting with clients, and preparing her case. She may be a hard worker; but, in the end, if she doesn't win any of those cases, we can't call her great—or even competent.

In a process-oriented school, how does one decide the merit of any particular instructional practice or paradigm? How do teachers determine the direction to focus their efforts and how to measure the success of those efforts? The answers here are clearly subjective and are commonly driven by the personal ideologies of the strongest influencers in the organization. Process-oriented influencers tend to minimize or ignore the results of formal assessments. They instead laud the strengths of subjective measures of success, which can be bent to support favored practices. While the results of benchmark and summative assessments are not the only data to be considered, ignoring the important information they provide can have a negative impact on outcomes at the school level.

One harmful result of this kind of atmosphere can be seen in schools where teachers feel highly successful because they implement practices that support the expected cultural norms. They do not even consider measuring their success against levels of student achievement. Another unconstructive result of a process-oriented environment is teachers who become highly frustrated by never knowing how to please their administrators. They feel as though success is a moving target, changing with the fickle whims of school leadership.

The Pressure to Please

If the teacher evaluation systems across the nation were overhauled to include student learning—which Race to the Top legislation demands—would the problem be solved? I believe the problem would only be alleviated if every school administrator decided to tell the truth when evaluating teachers. You see, under the new legislation, a teacher's evaluation will be based on a combination of student achievement data, as well as indicators relating to teacher skill and knowledge. Already, the Florida State Senate approved a bill that would include both in the evaluation process for new teachers.

> [Teachers] would work on one-year contracts and face dismissal if their students did not show learning gains on end-of-year exams for two years in any five-year period. For them, job security would be based solely on two factors: standardized scores and job reviews by principals. (Hafenbrack, 2010)

Although including student achievement in the evaluation process is a positive step in the evaluation process, the value of the process will still rest in the principal's ability to be honest about teacher effectiveness. In fact, I think everyone knows and would agree that's the key. But when leaders are put on the spot to act in a truthful manner, some are unprepared.

An experienced principal described a situation in which he was brought into a failing school to make big changes—fast. His charge was to ensure that teachers were teaching the district's curriculum, evaluate teachers honestly, and hold them accountable for student achievement, all in year one. Although he voiced concerns about changing too many things too fast, his boss insisted there was no time to go slow. But a few key teachers in the school welcomed none of these changes and quickly got the union involved. In the end, the principal was let go less than one year after his hire because the higher ups at the district office feared trouble with the union.

Opportunity for Reflection

Reflect upon your own faculty, specifically on who stands out as being ineffective. How have you rated them in the past? If the evaluation has been positive, why? What fears may have kept you from being honest?

In another situation, a new principal began to hold an ineffective teacher accountable and even got the teacher a district mentor to assist in the planning and instructional process. But by the end of the school year, the district mentor surprised the principal when she suggested that the teacher should be rated as meeting standards no matter how much the students had or had not learned—because of all the time he had put into the effort. **So, whether we are a leader at the district office or a school-based leader, why do we refuse to hold teachers accountable for student achievement?**

 ## Need for Acceptance vs. Fear of Rejection

Our old brain senses the fear from our middle brain, where the limbic system resides, and promptly makes the decision to avoid the dangerous behavior— in this case, holding teachers accountable. We think that doing so will create a staff who hates us. So instead, we make excuses as to why we can't confront the problems before us. According to Todd Whitaker (2003), "When we hesitate to . . . take up an issue with a teacher, it's easy to use the rationale, 'I don't want to hurt their feelings,' when it is really our own feelings that we want to protect" (p. 64–5). When we make decisions to keep people happy with us, the outcome is rarely what we're looking for. It's impossible to keep everyone happy with us all the time.

One administrator recounted a time when she overcame the fear of rejection to hold a team of teachers accountable for student achievement. This was a team of experienced teachers who had been together on the same team in the same school for a very long time. While many staff members viewed them as bullies, this team had established a strong following in the school community. So when the students on their team continued to fall behind and the principal began to set expectations, the teachers enlisted the help of their powerful community. It didn't take long for this principal's office to be barraged by unhappy parents, unleashing their outrage and demanding that the teachers be left alone. The members of the board of education, along with the superintendent also received unhappy communications from this outspoken group. This principal had been rejected by the school community.

 ## Need for Respect vs. Fear of Judgment

Accountability is a tough concept to introduce into a field in which workers are already overworked and underpaid. Teachers work long hours, buy supplies with their own money, and in many districts, hardly make enough money to live in the areas in which they serve. Most teachers get into the field and stay for altruistic reasons. They, on the whole, are well-intentioned, hard workers. That's why it's difficult to now come along and say, "Okay. I know you're already working long hours and your frustrated with the many requirements and challenges of the job. But that's not really good enough anymore. Now, you also have to find ways to make every child you teach reach or exceed grade-level standards." Drawing judgment from your staff would be a guarantee. You see, because most teachers haven't been fairly compensated for what they've done in the past and because people outside the profession have begun making tougher demands, raising the expectations to include accountability can seem unfair. And whether justified or not, these feelings of injustice are destructive to the school. When people believe they are being treated unfairly, a victim mentality develops. This situation is described by Roger Connors, Tom Smith, and Craig Hickman (2004) in *The Oz Principal*:

> Rather than face reality, sufferers of this malady oftentimes begin ignoring or pretending not to know about their accountability, denying their responsibility, blaming others for their predicament, citing confusion as a reason for inaction, asking others to tell them what to do, claiming that they can't do it, or just waiting to see if the situation will miraculously resolve itself. (p. 10)

Connors et al. characterizes these behaviors as "below the line," versus behaviors that embrace accountability known as "above the line." Below the line behaviors from teachers (and the feelings behind them) keep principals from creating a culture of accountability in their buildings.

As one animated secondary school principal explained, being judged by your staff is a hard thing to handle. You have to ask yourself if it's really worth it or not—especially when some of your teachers have been allowed to be ineffective for 15, 20, or even 30 years. And when principals realize that they may only be placed in a particular building for five years or so, it's much safer and more pleasant to just relax into a comfortable dysfunction with staff. The other, less scary option to accountability is administratively transferring an ineffective teacher. But it's hard to feel authentically good about yourself as a leader when you've passed your problem on to someone else to do damage to their students.

Ironically though, a leader's conscience may not only provide motivation to do the right thing, it can also lead to the avoidance of accountability. You see, if school leaders don't feel they would be able to improve student achievement as a teacher, they may feel morally wrong in asking it of their teachers. Hence, self-efficacy is an essential prerequisite to being an effective and fearless school leader.

So, what is the prescription to squelch the fears of holding teachers responsible for student learning?

Antidote: Develop Courage by Empowering Teachers—Hold Them Accountable for Student Achievement

Set Your Intention

In order to overcome the fears associated with developing a culture of accountability, school leaders must change their focus of concern from themselves to the higher concern of students and their achievement. The solution to our biological and emotional tendencies is spiritual in nature. We must remember our soul's purpose of impacting students and bravely forge ahead to rectify our broken education system.

Michelle Rhee, the embattled Washington, D.C. Schools Chancellor, took the city by storm when she proposed a new evaluation system that would do away with tenure and give effective teachers the opportunity to double their salaries. Whether or not you are a fan of Rhee, it is important that we respect the perilous stand she took. She fired ineffective teachers and administrators, facing derision from many stakeholders, especially the teachers' union. My suspicion is that Rhee knew exactly what she was getting herself into when she took the actions she did, but made the conscious decision to forgo job security and the need for acceptance in order to benefit thousands of students who could not themselves fight for the right to a good education. She risked everything and, in the end, resigned before she lost her job for it. But Rhee, who now finds herself on the world stage, is finally getting the accolades she deserves in the recent documentary, *Waiting for Superman*. Gathering the moral courage to set this new intention may not end in celebrity for you or even glean a word of praise. But it will provide a powerful life direction.

So ask yourself, what have I been put here to do? How will I respond to the crisis in achievement that has been put in front of me? When we work only to keep our jobs and get that paycheck at the end of the week, we remain emotionally and spiritually unfulfilled. We act out of fear and self-preservation. But when we view our daily work as an opportunity to fulfill our own destiny as agents of positive change, our satisfaction and authentic sense of self-worth increase dramatically. No longer an insignificant individual, we become worthy players in an education movement that will improve the lives of countless children in this country. Staying in this mindset, school leaders can not only tolerate risk, but will view it as only an afterthought.

One comfort is the truth that good teachers already know what their jobs are. They take responsibility for student learning. In *What Great Principals Do* Differently, Todd Whitaker (2003) shares a dialogue he's had with many teachers over the years, along with the predictable answers:

> If the best teacher in a school gives a quiz, test, or homework assignment and the kids do poorly on it (and, as we are all aware, this can happen to the best of us), whom does she blame?
> *The predictable answer: Herself.*
> Now, if the worst teacher in a school gives a quiz, test, or homework assignment and the kids do poorly on it (and, as we just acknowledged, this can happen to the best of us), whom does she blame?
> *Typical answers: The kids, or the parents, or the administration ("If we had some discipline around here maybe we could teach these kids something"), or last year's teachers, or drugs, or MTV, or . . . (p. 14)*

All teachers deserve to know what their job really is and how they will be deemed either successful or unsuccessful. And no matter how few indicators on your district's evaluation tool align to student achievement, you can make growth in learning the basis for what is considered success in your building. Let's face it: the evaluation process in many places is but a rubber stamp anyway. The real evaluation process increases accountability and it takes place every day of the school year, with every teacher conversation, every student assessment, and every piece of student work.

Build Trust

Shared Accountability

We're in this together. According to Connors et al. (2004), "Organizational results come from collective, not individual, activity. Hence, when an organization fails to perform well, it represents, ultimately, a collective or shared failure" (p. 49). This notion of shared responsibility, discussed in Chapter 4, is crucial to holding teachers accountable for student learning. Teacher empowerment does not mean that the principal can wipe his hands of involvement in the learning process. Just the opposite is true, in fact. While teachers will be encouraged to use data to select and monitor effective classroom practices, they will most definitely seek the input of school leadership. Singular responsibility is lonely, painful, and inadequate to build expertise throughout the school.

The Uncontrollables

Along with the trust-building strategies presented in previous chapters designed to support teachers, an essential component to helping teachers accept responsibility for student learning is acknowledging the uncontrollable. Connors et al. (2004) reminds us of this: "Don't hold everyone accountable for everything all the time . . . do understand the uncontrollables" (p. 173). This doesn't mean that school leaders should allow teachers to make excuses as to why students aren't learning. What it does acknowledge is that in education, as in business, there are certain circumstances beyond our control. And we must make the decision not to worry about them—and then help our teachers do the same. For instance, if a particular student has terrible attendance, we can investigate why, meet with the family, work on our own relationship with the student, get the pupil personnel officer and guidance counselor involved, etc. But in the end, if we can't get the student in school, his achievement will suffer. So we need to take this kind of information into account when helping teachers take responsibility. Teachers need to know that we don't expect them to do the impossible. Instead, help them to focus on what they *can* influence through their everyday instructional practices.

Campaign: Identify the Pain and the Gain

One of the biggest sources of **pain** that teachers in non-accountable schools face is the lack of empowerment. They are told what to do, how to do it, and are given too little time to get it all done. The focus of school leadership is making sure that all teachers are "reading from the hymnal," following the lock-step structure for instruction that has been put into place. No teacher would want to accept accountability in that kind of controlling environment. Changing the culture means empowering teachers. And accountability equals empowerment—a big **gain**.

Clear Teachers' Plates

So tell your teachers with your words and your actions that their job is to ensure student learning—that all of their students should either meet or exceed grade-level standards—period. Everything else is minutia. All of the other details that have to be done will get done, but we won't waste our time talking about them—or complaining about them. Our time, our conversations, and our focus will be achievement. This is the time to **clear teachers'**

plates of as much as possible that is unrelated to that priority. Find ways to diminish or reassign administrative tasks to other staff and downplay required initiatives that do not directly impact achievement.

Give Back Control

Now, let go of the rest and allow your teachers be the professionals they can and want to be. Besides clearing teachers' plates, the other requisite to increasing accountability is **giving them the professional freedom to choose the instructional strategies that will increase student achievement.** Connors et al. (2004) writes about the positive aspects of accountability, stating, "Correctly understood and properly applied, accountability empowers people with a new sense of control and influence over their circumstances so they can achieve the results they desire" (p. 164). One of the unfortunate effects of the culture of high stakes assessment has been principals who hold tightly to complete control of the educational process within the school. The national, state, and district levels already tell us what to teach and dictate minimum levels of proficiency. Many principals then dictate how the curriculum is to be taught. What's left for teachers? They have no control. It would be akin to walking into the doctor's office and instead of being seen by your doctor, you're seen by your doctor, along with a room full of people. They tell him what tests to run, what prescriptions to give, and then blame him when you don't get better. No, in your school, teachers will be free to teach, to select their strategies, and then to measure their own effectiveness.

Show Clear Contrast

Remember to keep the old brain in mind when communicating your new intention by showing contrast between what your school is becoming and what it once was. Unlike schools where teachers are told how to teach, in this school, teachers will be treated as professionals. Teachers will be expected to select instructional practices to try, implement them, and then evaluate the result to make new adjustments. There will exist a constant cycle of Plan, Do, Study, Act until all students have met or exceeded grade-level standards. Students will succeed and all teachers will be highly skilled practitioners. This Plan, Do, Study, Act improvement cycle mirrors Connors et al.'s (2004) "above the line" behaviors of accountability—"See It, Own It, Solve It, Do It." The power in this cycle is that it calls for teachers to acknowledge that both the current strengths and the current deficits in student learning are a direct result of their instruction. It requires and rewards teachers for having "a level of ownership that includes making, keeping, and answering for personal commitments" (p. 47).

> ## *Opportunity for Reflection*
>
> Reflect upon what you control in your school vs. what your teachers control. Do teachers control enough to be fairly held accountable for student learning?

Build Expertise Together

Implement Pacing Conferences

In his book *No Excuses*, Samuel Casey Carter (2001) writes about the importance of schools working together toward a common purpose: "High expectations are one thing—the relentless pursuit of excellence is another. Tangible and unyielding goals are the focus for high-performing schools . . . great schools set hard and fast goals that the whole school must strive to obtain" (p. 9). Compelling Conversations, as described by Thomasina Piercy (2006) in her book by the same name, provide the perfect forum to have data conversations that change instructional practices and increase accountability. I was fortunate enough to have Piercy as a professional colleague during the time she was developing the concept of compelling conversations, and therefore was able to experiment with the practice at my school. These structured discussions empower teachers to pace out expected student achievement throughout the year, which is why they can also be known as pacing conferences or achievement meetings. Whether it's tracking reading levels or tracking mastery of curriculum objectives, the point is to closely analyze and respond to student learning early instead of waiting until end of year or end of course assessments are given. In this way, appropriate instructional changes can be implemented early and student success ensured.

As school leaders, we may not be able to change the formal evaluation process utilized by our district, but we can build structures within our schools that support accountability. By using data to set and monitor achievement goals, we can help our teachers take responsibility for student learning. The following is a distilled adaptation of the process I used at my school. The results were overwhelmingly positive.

Step 1: Communicating Current Instructional Levels. The process begins at the start of the school year when teachers are given data pertaining to each student's standing in relation to grade-level standards, e.g., instructional reading levels. The data should also be presented in such a way that alerts teachers to who is functioning below, on, and above grade level. Visuals such as class pie graphs or bar graphs are highly effective. Teachers can then use the Student Chart (Figure 6.1) to record specific levels of student functioning. This is the level at which the current teacher will begin instruction. Similar charts can be used to backward map progress in other subject areas suitable evidence of student learning has been determined.

In other content areas and at the high school level, this step would involve meeting with departments at the beginning of the year, quarter, or semester to discuss students who struggled to meet course expectations.

Step 2: Setting Goals for Each Student. Teachers then set end-of-year academic goals for each student based on grade-level standards. The rule of thumb is: each student must make at least one year's growth during the school year, ending the year at least on grade level. For students beginning the year above grade level, they too should make at least one year's growth. Students functioning below grade level must make more than one year's growth; their learning must be accelerated. If not, how will they ever catch up? Most teachers of below grade level students set their goals at a year and a half's growth. The principal should participate in the step of setting these end-of-year goals for students. One way to accomplish this is to have the teacher set tentative goals and then meet with administration to review them together. Some teachers may want help in selecting appropriate goals for certain students, especially those significantly above or below grade level.

In other content areas and school levels, teachers would set an end-of-course goal for each student. This goal could involve performance on the end-of-course exam or assessment. In order to set an appropriate goal, teachers would analyze past student data (Step 1). If teachers are responsible for a large number of students, making this step too cumbersome, then focusing on struggling students would make the process more realistic.

Step 3: Backward-Mapping the Year. After the end of year or course goal has been set, teachers backward-map each month or quarter of the school year to determine where students must be along the way. At the secondary level, divide the course into three or four equal time periods. After each of these, an assessment would be administered. A common formative assessment for gauging progress must be identified as a part of this step. Whenever possible, make use of any required district assessments that teachers must already give. The interim goals developed are then written into the student map.

Step 4: Discussing Student Progress Toward Goals. During the school year, the principal then meets with individual teachers, grade-level teams, or departments at predetermined times to check on the progress of students. I always prefer meeting with the grade-level team as a whole, due to the

FIGURE 6.1 Student Map–Middle/Elementary

Teacher:	School Year:								
Incoming Students	Incoming State Results	Last Year's Teacher Recommendations	1st Quarter	2nd Quarter	3rd Quarter	4th Quarter	State GOAL	Projected State Results	Teacher Recommendation

Number of students performing at Mastery or Above: ___ ___ ___
Number of students performing Below Mastery: ___ ___ ___

From Piercy, *Compelling Conversations*. Copyright 2006 Advanced Learning Press. Reprinted with permission of Advanced Learning Press.

learning opportunities and sense of shared accountability the conversations offer. If certain students are not attaining their quarterly goals, then conversations take place in order to identify roadblocks to student progress and find solutions. In these solutions lie the instructional changes that must take place. During the conversations, the principal's role is to participate in problem-solving with the team, asking thoughtful questions, and seeking doable solutions. This is the heart of shared accountability. Some questions I found helpful were:

- ◆ "Why do you think this group of students is stuck at this instructional level?"
- ◆ "If time and resources were unlimited, what would you do to move this child forward?"
- ◆ "Are you noticing any striking strengths or weaknesses with this group of students?"
- ◆ "If this child were your only student, how would you spend the day educating him?"

These questions usually helped teachers free up their thinking in order to identify areas of student weakness, along with strategies they'd like to implement to address the need. It also allowed the group of teachers to find similarities and differences in their personal instructional strengths. Most importantly, it helped to identify constraints that the processes of traditional schooling tend to reinforce. The team could then think divergently about daily scheduling, student grouping, and instructional practices to find ways to give students what they needed. The discussion always worked to open up conversations that should be happening in schools, but oftentimes didn't. Due to invisible barriers, we hesitate to talk about what's actually happening in classrooms, keeping many instructional practices private. Some questions to spur this needed dialogue are:

- ◆ "What opportunities do students have to evaluate their own work?"
- ◆ "What does your daily whole group reading instruction look like?"
- ◆ "What do you teach in small group versus whole group and why?"
- ◆ "What scaffolding tools do you use to teach math reasoning?"
- ◆ "How and when are you teaching writing conventions?"

Teachers always learn a tremendous amount about their colleagues' daily practice through these discussions. They can also realize what practices they've perhaps been inadvertently overlooking and begin to implement them.

Besides helping teachers develop action plans, the principal is also able to offer financial assistance for any needed materials, or work to rearrange schedules of support staff if needed. Remember, this should be a non-judgmental activity. It is important for the principal to show trust in the teachers by expressing a belief in their ability to directly and rapidly increase achievement in struggling students.

These pacing conferences and the "compelling conversations" (Piercy, 2006) within them change traditional schooling processes. Normally, teachers would begin the school year by assessing students to determine the beginning instructional level. Then instruction would continue throughout the course of the year, the teacher hoping for the best. At the end of the year, the teacher would record the ending instructional level on the articulation card for next year's teacher. Little thought would be given to how much growth the student was able to make in the course of the school year. And if some teachers did analyze student growth, it would be too late to take any corrective action. Even in a school where growth was measured throughout the school year at selected times, teachers would be unable to recognize a student falling behind without the help of interim goals. I once worked with a teacher who was proud that her student had made one reading level's growth in half a year. "He's making progress!" she exclaimed. What she wasn't aware of is the student should have made four level's growth by that time in order to be on grade level by the end of the school year.

Pacing conferences at the elementary and secondary level allow teachers to begin instruction with the end result in mind. Achievement is backward mapped and monitored in intervals throughout the year or course. In this way, precious time is not wasted before teachers realize that particular students may not progress to grade level or course standards. Pacing conferences offer accountability within a supportive team environment. When a student is found to be in academic trouble, grade-level teachers or departments share the burden of the responsibility, share their professional expertise, work together to devise an intervention plan, and allocate human and capital resources equitably.

Attempting to utilize interim assessments without implementing pacing conferences will have limited success. Focused goals based on grade-level/course standards, along with specific and simple action plans for struggling students, will ensure success.

Pacing Conference: Take One

I can recall a fear-provoking grade-level pacing conference, one that I won't soon forget: It was the end of January, one of the most significant times to analyze data. And the purpose of this pacing conference was to check mid-year progress of our first grade students. The young teachers gathered quickly in the conference room at their appointed time. Looking back now, I realize they were all behaving a bit anxiously. But that day, I didn't notice. Arriving to the conference room ten minutes late, my mind raced with remnants of a suspension, a phone conversation with an angry parent, and a disagreement between two teachers. The first-grade team began sharing their reading data in turns, and it wasn't until about 10 minutes into the meeting that the words traveling through my ears to my brain finally sounded an alarm. My numbness wore off to the pain of hearing that nearly a third of the first graders had not met their January goal, meaning that they were below grade level. My eyes engaged theirs. Uneasy, each teacher explained that they were doing everything they knew how to do for their students, and were frustrated with the lack of progress. On the inside, my stress level grew with each passing minute, but I knew I needed to remain calm. After each teacher had shared the bad news, I thanked them all for their hard work and dedication—and I meant it. These were talented young people who took their responsibility seriously. Quickly, I ended the meeting.

This experience is the reason why so many school leaders fear data and fear holding their teachers accountable. When the data is out in the open for all to see and it's bad, it must be addressed. This puts principals on the hot seat, making them feel as though they need to have all the answers. They know they must fix it, but how? It's much easier to avoid looking at data through the school year. Ignorance is bliss. But I had already opened this can of worms. So, my assistant principal and I closed ourselves in my office and allowed ourselves a few minutes of panic. How could this have happened? Everything seemed so on track. What's going on? Soon, our questions became more focused.

- ◆ What is holding the students back from attaining their goals?
- ◆ Is it the same problem in each classroom?
- ◆ How can we find out more? What can we do?
- ◆ No, what *are* we going to do?

The first thing we did was call a meeting with all of the resource staff who serviced first-grade students. The meeting included the special education teacher, the reading specialist, two instructional assistants, the guidance counselor, the assistant principal, and me. The purpose of the meeting was to share the alarming data coming from the first-grade team and to listen to any information they could share regarding the first graders they serviced. I was clear with them that I needed their help and support. And that together, I knew we could solve this problem. As I began divulging the upsetting news, their concern was immediately apparent. Gathered around the data sheets, asking questions of me and of one another, the resource staff got to work. I don't know exactly how to explain what happened next, except to say that the conversation became synergistic. We met for an hour and left with a plan. I knew I'd be able to sleep that night.

Plan:
   1. Have another pacing conference with the first-grade teachers. This time, the resource staff would attend as well. This conference would be an extended half-day meeting to give adequate time for problem-solving.
   2. Collaboratively analyze the formative data we had for programmatic weaknesses.
   3. Put a plan into place that every first-grade teacher would begin implementing immediately.

The next day, I scheduled a follow-up pacing conference with the first-grade team. I met with the team leader and explained to him that I was alarmed at the data his team had presented. This was no surprise to him. I explained the plan to him and asked that he help guide his team both during the conference and after the conference during implementation.

Pacing Conference: Take Two

A few days later, we gathered for the second pacing conference. A slight tension was apparent at the beginning, but quickly dissipated as I explained the goal of the meeting and shared my confidence in the team's ability to collaboratively come up with solutions that would help their students make quick progress. I stated that the resource staff was included in the meeting to provide extra support, lend expertise, and to be part of the solution. More importantly, they were responsible for the first graders' success, too.

This time the teachers brought the actual assessments, instead of the scores. We decided to analyze the latest running record for each student in order to uncover what weakness held the student back from moving on to the next level. The data was organized on a chart drawn by hand on large butcher paper. The categories included: phonics/phonemic awareness, sight words, comprehension, vocabulary/background knowledge, and strategy use. We split the huge stack of running records among us and began the analysis. As we read each assessment and determined which area held the student back,

FIGURE 6.2 Tally Chart

Phonics/Phonetic Awareness	Sight Words	Comprehension	Vocabulary	Strategy Use
〤〤〤 〤〤〤 〤〤〤 〤|||	〤〤〤 〤〤〤 〤〤〤 〤〤〤 〤〤|||	〤〤〤 〤〤〤 〤|||	〤〤〤 〤〤|||	〤〤〤 〤〤|||

we placed a tally mark under that category on the chart. About an hour into our analysis, the results were striking. The large majority of our tallies ended up in "phonics" and "sight words." Upon completion of our analysis, we found that the early trend remained true (see Figure 6.2).

The last portion of our meeting was then dedicated to the question, "What are we going to do about this?" To address the phonics deficit, we developed an instructional plan that each teacher would use whole group and with their leveled reading groups every day. The reading specialist and special education teacher were invaluable during this part of the meeting. Their expertise in how to effectively teach phonics was absolutely necessary here to ensure that the components of our plan were strong enough to move students forward quickly.

We then developed a grade-wide sight word program to address the sight word deficit. After each classroom teacher felt comfortable with their part of the implementation plan, the resource staff offered their help. Students who were at highest academic risk were given an intervention by one of the resource staff members. We chose the intervention and made sure it complemented the plan that the classroom teachers were to use. Before the meeting ended I expressed my pride and gratitude in what we had accomplished together in a few hours. I also made it clear that if everyone did their part, this plan should work. But . . . if it didn't, no one would be blamed. Instead, if in a month, we didn't see improvement, we would get back together and change the plan. Emotional support and an easily understood and executable plan are crucial here in order for teachers to overcome the fear of implementing a new plan. Connors et al. (2004) reminds us, "Fear of the risk of failing can so debilitate many people that they build walls between *Solve It* and *Do It*. However, only by accepting the risk can you penetrate the walls and break down all the barriers to success" (p. 135). Everyone left the meeting with a renewed sense of confidence, purpose and urgency. Just a month later, we saw gains in achievement. And by the end of the school year, almost all students were on grade level in reading. Shared accountability between principal and faculty

Opportunity for Reflection

What structures are currently in place to help teachers track student progress throughout the year toward grade-level proficiency? How can compelling conversations be used in your school to increase accountability?

How can you show your faculty and staff that you share in the accountability for student learning?

How can you develop your teachers' confidence in their ability to increase achievement? What opportunities and experiences will you plan?

How will pacing conferences/compelling conversations impact the way you determine teacher effectiveness? How could it impact teacher evaluation?

had led to a strong sense of teacher efficacy. They had become empowered professionals.

Note: It is important to note that we led the classroom teachers in developing their instructional plans first. Then the resource staff offered help in providing interventions. This decision helped classroom teachers understand the truth that their own instruction was going to have the biggest impact on student achievement. They also received the message that we trusted them to do this. The outcome of the meeting would have been very different had we started by planning interventions for resource teachers to implement. Always remember to build efficacy in your classroom teachers. They must believe that they can improve the achievement of all students in their classrooms.

7

Fearless Decision: Holding High Expectations for Student Achievement

As a new administrator in a new school district, I spent time during my first month talking with various stakeholders, including the principal, staff, and parents, becoming familiar with the school's culture. Many of the comments I heard celebrated the school's excellence. This perception surprised me. As a part of the interview process, I had researched the school's performance on the high-stakes assessment, and its results were concerning. So when I began speaking with staff and members of the community, I expected to hear anxieties and suggestions, not accolades. I had to find out what these comments were based upon.

I asked myself, in comparison to *what* is this school excellent? What *was* immediately evident was the hard work and dedication of the school's staff. They were truly pouring all of their energy into helping students learn every day. I also found supportive parents who valued education and supported the school through volunteering, reading to their children at home, as well as helping them with homework assignments each night. The effort of the entire school community was excellent. But for some reason, it wasn't translating into achievement. My introductory investigation took me to the cumulative files housed in the front office. I wondered just how successful students could be in their classes if they weren't achieving proficiency on the minimum state standards. So I took a deep breath as I made the decision to delve into the muddy arena of report card grades. After hours of studying grades and reading comments on report cards, I had an "a-ha moment"—here's the excellence!

Of the hundreds of report cards I pored over, I found only five Cs and one D. All other report cards were composed of mostly As with a few interspersed Bs. No wonder all stakeholders believed in the "excellence" of this school. It was there in black and white for all to see and believe. I knew then that there were some difficult conversations ahead of me if we were to align state expectations with our teachers' expectations.*

All Students Can Learn

How many times have we all heard this line? It is regularly stated by school leaders with the conviction of Winston Churchill in his famous wartime radio broadcasts. But how much conviction does it really take to make this statement? Truly, who doesn't accept that all human beings have the capacity to learn? The belief in this sentiment does not a brave man make.

What would up the ante is putting some metrics to the statement. To what level can all students learn? Congress answered this question resolutely in 2002 with the No Child Left Behind legislation, mandating that all diploma-bound students meet grade-level proficiency by 2014. But government mandates do not have the power to change the hearts and minds of those working in our schools on a daily basis.

While the federal government and the U.S. Department of Education set the new standard years ago, many schools have continued to struggle in answering the question, "To what level can all of our diploma-bound students learn?" Kids are different, right? So many schools choose a well-meaning, yet nebulous and quite dangerous measure: All students can learn to their potential. Which begs the question, "How do we know the innate potential of each student?" Some rely on aptitude tests and the like, but I don't think I need to provide examples here of famous Americans who far exceeded the minimal potential their teachers saw in them.

As stated earlier, educators must acknowledge that there are students who, due to medical trauma or other causes, have severely impaired cognitive ability and are non-diploma bound—an alternative path through public school. This situation can explain why educators feel comfortable with the term *potential*. It does take into consideration the varied abilities of students. But for those headed to college and into this country's work force, the term *potential* can do harm with its unintended consequences of low expectations—especially for minority, special needs, and disadvantaged students. Who are

*From McCabe, The Myth of Excellence in Suburban Schools. *ASCD Express*. Copyright 2008 ASCD. Reprinted with permissions from ASCD.

we to decide what a student's potential will be? And what latent cultural biases might impact that decision?

One principal shared the story of a math teacher who, after working with any of the students in the free lunch program, would exclaim in her highest pitch, "I didn't think you could do it!" I can relate to this story. Growing up in a rough neighborhood, I got used to teachers who didn't think my classmates and I could accomplish much. So for the most part, school work was easy. Teachers were more interested in making sure we behaved appropriately than in providing a rigorous learning experience. But there were a few exceptions . . . one was my twelfth-grade English teacher. We all knew she was tough, assigning challenging learning tasks and refusing to accept sub-par work. But I didn't come to a full appreciation of the situation until I attended the Senior Thesis Symposium held at a local college. There, select students in advanced English from across the district shared their senior theses with one another and with high school and college instructors. As I sat there listening to other students present, it became obvious that our theses were much more sophisticated and complex than those from other schools. The sense of pride in my own capabilities, along with gratitude for my teacher, surfaced that day—a feeling I've remembered for many years. But many aren't so lucky.

The Cover-Up

Lowering Rigor

I once heard a story about a hopeful young man who, having just graduated from his urban high school with a full scholarship, began his first semester at a four-year college. But after only two weeks of attending classes, he was lost, unable to follow the lectures or begin his assignments. He lacked the prerequisite skills and knowledge to build understanding of the content being taught. Shocked and in disbelief, he was forced to drop all classes and reenroll in remedial courses. These were just what he needed, and in time he was able to successfully complete all courses of study in order to graduate. When asked to comment on the situation he faced in starting his college career, he shared one regret. He wished that someone had told him that the 4.0 GPA he earned at his high school didn't mean the same thing as the 4.0 GPA earned at the high school 15 miles away. A young man who had reached the peak of "excellence" in his neighborhood high school couldn't tread water in entry-level college courses.

In their zeal to help students experience success in their classes, some educators lower the academic expectations of the course. In the minds of these helpful teachers, lowering the bar ensures high levels of student "success." It's a benevolent cover-up for low achievement. And oftentimes, school leaders are unable to recognize these lowered standards in particular classes, especially if the class is in an unfamiliar content. Using signposts such student performance on SAT, AP, state, and local assessments can provide guidance. If nearly all students are receiving As in an AP course, yet only half can pass the AP exam, there's a problem to investigate. When leaders discover that their school has lowered levels of rigor, they will have to decide whether or not to confront it.

Inflating Student Grades

Another familiar and well-meaning practice used to help everyone look and feel successful is padding grades. Everything from class participation to extra credit projects to bringing in requested school supplies can pump up student grades, enabling a student who isn't achieving course outcomes to receive high grades. The American epidemic of flawed grading was captured in Marzano's (2000) 1996 McREL study in which teachers were asked to identify attributes other than subject matter content mastery used when assigning grades to students. Identified were "effort, behavior, cooperation and attendance" (p. 4). One principal described the day she found a teacher offering percentage points in exchange for packages of tissues. Students were able earn extra points for the number of boxes they contributed to the classroom, increasing grades by means that had absolutely nothing to do with mastery of course content.

Opportunity for Reflection

Reflect upon the academic expectations in your school. Are they appropriate or too low? Are they different for particular subgroups?

Are the report card grades in your school an accurate reflection of student mastery of course concepts? How much of a student's grade is influenced by compliance?

What are your staff's beliefs about the level to which students can learn?

Another school leader told of a high school teacher who assigned mostly long-term group projects that were completed both at home and at school. If students completed each part of the assignment, worked cooperatively with their group, and turned in the final product, they received an A. Needless to say, it was pretty easy to earn an A—just comply. And most of his students *did* receive As. Both parents and students loved him. And his principal kept him.

If, starting immediately, teachers were to assign grades based solely on student mastery of rigorous course content, there would be scores of students failing out of "good" schools. Students would be stunned by the demands of meeting new competencies and teachers would struggle to teach students to mastery. Parents would be up in arms. Reporters would be asking questions. And school leaders would have to answer. Grade inflation halts this state of emergency—along with the stress and fear that accompanies it.

Why Do We Make the Decision to Hold Low Expectations for Student Achievement?

 Need for Mastery vs. Fear of Failure

At the core of why we hold low expectations for students as a whole, as well as for some subgroups, is the fact that it is the safe thing to do. And these low expectations soon become the norm around the country, rather than the exception, being passed down from one experienced educator to her student teacher and so on, so that Generation Y educators cannot recognize the diminished intellectual demands that many educators around them have created and nurtured. Mediocrity becomes institutionalized. To wake many teachers and leaders up to this reality would take transplanting them into a school which is in stark contrast to their own—one with collective responsibility for setting and maintaining high standards of achievement for all students. This abrupt transition would cause immediate fear and anxiety. Why? Either we don't believe that our students have the capacity to meet and exceed grade-level/course standards, or we don't believe we can teach well enough to get them there.

The Students Just Can't Do It

One of the unintended consequences of implementing special education law within our schools is that it can reinforce the notion that if a student "isn't getting it" when the rest are, there must be something wrong with him.

In the minds of many educators, special education neatly explains student difficulties and relieves the regular educator of responsibility for the troubles.

I taught it + He didn't get it = A problem within the student

Many teachers are satisfied if 70% or 80% of their students are able to master the content being taught in any particular day, week, or marking period, believing it natural for a portion of the class to have difficulty. Therefore, the teacher doesn't examine her own instructional program for flaws or gaps. The teacher may try reteaching the material, but if the student still experiences problems, oftentimes he is referred to the special education team for screening. If the student doesn't qualify for services—and many do not—he can struggle for years, receiving satisfactory (albeit false) grades, but falling further and further behind, the victim of poor instruction. Basic mistakes that contribute to poor instruction include:

◆ The failure to align instruction with the written curriculum (grade/ course standards)
◆ The failure to teach concepts in a systematic, logical sequence
◆ The failure to actively involve students in authentic learning experiences
◆ The failure to provide direct, explicit instruction
◆ The failure to set clear objectives for learning and then measure that learning daily, allowing the data to guide instruction

The cumulative effect of these breakdowns is devastating to students. In a study on achievement gain using the Tennessee Value-Added Assessment System, researchers "found that students taught by the least effective (bottom quintile of) teachers for three consecutive years displayed average achievement gains of 29%. In contrast, students taught by the most effective teachers gained 83%" (National Governor's Association, 2010). June Rivers, an educational researcher at SAS, discovered "that if a student has an ineffective teacher, a learning deficit can almost always be measured four years later—even if they have had several highly effective teachers afterwards" (Reeder, 2005).

If educators do not improve their practice in order to reach all students each year, pockets of children, especially disadvantaged and minority students, move through the primary grades falling further and further behind. They are deprived of good instruction for too long. Upon entering the intermediate grades, special education testing reveals a discrepancy between ability and achievement, qualifying these students for services. These are the children who are unfairly labeled as learning disabled, when in reality, the root cause of their difficulty is not organic at all. They have been instructionally disabled by the school. To accept and even expect portions of the student population to struggle—without professional self-examination—is the epitome of low expectations.

For those who don't believe it is realistic to hold high standards of achievement across the board, just take a look at what's being done around the country:

♦ At the Seed School, an urban public charter school in Washington, D.C., 96% of students have been accepted to four-year colleges and universities (U.S. Department of Education, 2006).

♦ The Gateway High School in San Francisco, a public charter school with a 25% special education population and a 33% free and reduced meals population, boasts a 95% graduation rate (U.S. Department of Education, 2006).

♦ At Watson Williams School, a rural elementary school in Utica, NY where 96% of its students are eligible for free and reduced meals, 100% of fourth graders met or exceeded proficiency in mathematics and 95% of fourth graders met or exceeded proficiency in reading on the state assessment (U.S. Department of Education, 2009).

♦ At Routh Roach Elementary School in Garland, Texas, a culturally diverse school where 45% of students have limited English proficiency and 61% of students are eligible for free and reduced meals, 100% of fifth grade students met or exceeded proficiency in math and 90% of fifth grade students met or exceeded proficiency in reading on the state assessment (U.S. Department of Education, 2009).

The list goes on and on. It is very possible to hold high expectations and meet them. The evidence is all around us, in all parts of the country, with all kinds of students.

Therefore, if we acknowledge the success stories and make the mental and emotional leap to believe it is possible for all kinds of students to meet and exceed grade-level standards, then we are left with the question of our own efficacy. Do we believe we have the power to teach to mastery?

I Just Can't Do It

It's easy for educators to doubt their own abilities—especially when students are impacted by so many factors beyond the school's control. This self-doubt is rooted in the real-life difficulties and past failures that every educator has experienced over the years with specific students. While not beneficial to anyone, this negative emotion is powerful enough to spur self-protective impulses and beliefs.

Another cause of self-doubt rests with the educational establishment itself—the unintended consequences of the system legally put into place to help children, the special education system. While special education policies and procedures have helped countless students get the help they needed, it has simultaneously disempowered a generation of educators. Let's examine what many teachers experience when a student isn't keeping up.

1. A child isn't learning at the expected rate.
2. His young teacher makes use of the pre-referral processes available in her school. But in this case, her student still fails to make progress.
3. An IEP meeting is held. The teacher has the chance to share her concerns about the student's progress. The team decides to test. She then hears the special educator and school psychologist describe the unfamiliar tests that will be administered. The teacher realizes that she lacks much of the specialized knowledge and skill of her colleagues. There's much she doesn't know about the complex world of special education.
4. At a subsequent IEP meeting, the assessment results are explained and the teacher learns that the special educator, speech pathologist, and school psychologist recommend qualifying the student for special education services. Again, the teacher does not have knowledge of the tests used or their metrics. A draft IEP is presented, an intricate plan in legalese that sounds overwhelming. She struggles to fully comprehend much of what is shared and feels self-conscious about her lack of understanding. She signs the documents, not daring to ask the multitude of questions that would help her to clear some of the confusion she feels.
5. The student's new services begin. He is pulled out of the regular educator's classroom and seen by the special educator and speech pathologist several times per week. The classroom teacher perceives that she is incapable of meeting this child's needs. After all, she didn't understand much that happened during the IEP process. And now, special educators must service this student, providing instruction in a way that she obviously cannot. What the special educators do with the student each day remains a mystery to the teacher.
6. The classroom teacher gives up responsibility for this student's learning.
7. Another student in the teacher's class exhibits difficulty in learning. The teacher immediately asks for special education testing, fearfully knowing the student needs something that she cannot provide.

Thankfully, not every situation involving special education goes this way. But many do. The same process that is supposed to help struggling students oftentimes disenfranchises the educator that can make the most difference in the child's progress. You see, in almost all cases, the classroom teacher spends more time with the special needs student than do any of his other service providers. It is also the classroom teacher who best knows the course/grade outcomes that students must meet. Unfortunately, many special educators, while skilled in implementing specific programs and methodologies, do not understand the demands inherent in the district's curriculum. Moreover, some do not perceive their job as getting identified students back on track, able to meet grade-level standards, and out of the special education system as quickly as possible. Instead, countless students enter the special education factory, receive a new label that explains to educators why they can't succeed, and stay there forever, making the minimal expected progress.

Skilled classroom teachers are the keys to success for struggling students. Therefore, school leaders who choose to hold high expectations for student achievement must confront their own fear of failure, along with that of their regular educators, using the need for mastery as potent motivation to act.

Need for Acceptance vs. Fear of Rejection

To many school leaders, feeling good is more important than actually being good. Whether this accomplished by lowered standards or inflated grades, when students are receiving As and Bs in their classes, as a rule, the students feel good, their parents feel good, and the community at large feels good. This happy environment then keeps day-to-day school life calm for the educators involved and makes them feel accepted by the community. Teachers aren't questioned about student grades or asked to defend their practices. School leaders aren't asked to change report card grades or come up with intervention plans to keep students from failing. There is no pressure, no conflict, no bad feelings. Increased achievement expectations from teachers would mean scrutiny and rejection from parents. And if school leaders expressed a need for increased expectations, they would face rejection from both teachers and parents. I can share from personal experience that when particular students who previously received high grades begin to earn average or lower grades while adjusting to increased standards, it is not a pretty scene. As students and their parents struggle to adjust to new demands, some evaluate their new circumstances as unfair and reject school leaders.

At one school, parents were upset with the high expectations of one particular grade-level team who had made the tough decision at the beginning of the school year to increase rigor. They requested meetings with the

> ### *Opportunity for Reflection*
>
> How has the fear of failure impacted your own, as well as your teach-ers', expectations of student achievement?
> How has the fear of rejection influenced how honestly your teachers report student achievement? If honesty meant lower grades, how much support would you show?

administration and raised concerns at PTA meetings. At parent conferences, many questioned the teachers about the appropriateness of the daily rigor. When the state and local curriculum documents were analyzed together, parents could see that the new expectations were right on target and, in time, made efforts to support their children in meeting the standards. The question that remained was what had happened in the previous grade level? Should the rigor have been that drastically different in the two grades? The principal had a new investigation to begin—and more controversy ahead. So what is the solution to holding low expectations for student achievement?

Antidote: Make a Fearless Decision—Hold High Expectations for All Students Throughout the School

Set Your Intention

If teachers are to believe that all students can meet or exceed grade-level stan-dards, their leaders have to believe it first. Use the following steps to clear unhelpful attitudes blocking your ability to set a new intention:

Take Inventory
Administrators can begin by taking an honest inventory of their true beliefs about what is possible for students to achieve. Allow yourself to think back and remember experiences that have influenced these beliefs, especially the negative ones. It is a natural human tendency to disown or bury thoughts and feelings that may be considered wrong or bad. But repression doesn't make the thoughts go away. They still influence us, causing guilt and shame—an unproductive emotional place.

Acknowledge the Bad and the Ugly

Instead of repressing or denying them, try to acknowledge the negative thoughts and beliefs you hold. Show yourself some compassion and understanding for having gone through the experiences that caused this negativity. They were probably some trying, stressful times.

Distance Yourself

Then remind yourself that these old beliefs, now out of the shadows and into the light, don't have to be your current ones. After being acknowledged, old feelings, thoughts, and beliefs don't have to control or define you now. When you feel them bubbling up, recognize them as part of your professional history and know that the future does not have to be determined by the past. You are much broader and deeper than this segment of your thoughts.

Move Past the Negative

Remember the times when you and your staff were very successful with groups of students or individuals. Maybe it's the student who came to your school well below grade level, weighed down by family upheaval, and you were able to provide the stable environment and effective instruction to bring him up to grade level with his peers. Focus on the positive feeling this memory brings forward: pride, gratitude, etc.

Consider the Possibilities

If it has happened in the past, both for you and for others, it is certainly possible to hold high expectations for student learning and see them come to fruition in the future. This fact provides hope for the possibilities ahead. Allow yourself to consider what it would be like—feel like—to lead a school that insisted on excellence for its students and got it. Set this as your new intention in order to live and work with meaning and purpose.

Build Trust

Principal to Teacher

When standards are raised, there will be an adjustment period for all stakeholders. Although teachers will support students through the transition, it is normal for student grades to drop for a time. During this period, teachers need to be reassured that school leaders will support them through the parent questions, concerns, and even disapproval. Administrators and teachers must together commit to riding out the storm, resisting the urge to go back to the way things were in order to keep the peace.

Teacher to Teacher

In order to raise expectations for all students, general educators and special educators need to benefit from one another's expertise. This process begins by building relationships between them. Special educators should be brought up to date with the district's curriculum content and standards for each grade level or course. General educators should be given opportunities to become familiar with specialized instructional programs which have, in the past, been known only to special educators. Both groups should be brought together and given the message that it is a collective responsibility for all students to meet or exceed grade-level standards. Check the school's meeting schedule and make sure that there are designated weekly times for special educators to meet with regular educators, either individually or in grade-level teams, to plan together. Regular educators should understand what special educators are doing with students when they are pulled out for direct instruction. They should also know how to support and complement that specialized instruction in the classroom.

Campaign: Identify the Pain and the Gain

Fear of failure is the **pain** that holds most teachers back from holding high expectations for all students. They don't believe it's possible to achieve, so they refuse to reach for it. Share the message that **all** teachers will be developed, so they know how to meet the needs of struggling students. Classroom teachers won't have to rely on others to "fix" the student. The **gain** for all is that, through effective collaboration among teachers, students will meet grade-level standards. Showing teachers they can achieve this will lead to a **sense of mastery**. This process will empower the teachers who have felt disempowered, giving them a new **sense of purpose**.

In campaigning for higher expectations, school leaders must include parents and the community. Using platforms such as PTA meetings, newsletters, and Q and A sessions to help parents understand the grave implications of low expectations should increase their support through the sometimes painful process of raising expectations. Leaders who manage expectations through this time have far fewer parent complaints about teacher demands and changing report card grades.

Show Clear Contrast

Just as it helps leaders to see and hear about excellent schools, it assists teachers as well. Share the evidence of success from sources such as the 90/90/90 schools, where 90% or more of students were eligible for free or reduced lunch, 90% or more of students were from ethnic minority groups, and where 90% or more students achieved high academic standards. This research by Doug Reeves (2003) will convince anyone of what is possible when a school gets serious about its reason for being—high academic achievement for all. Contrast these 90/90/90 schools with those who are not succeeding. Your school or neighboring schools may be included in this comparison to personalize the analysis.

Build Expertise Together

In this section, three strategies will be suggested in order to help your school take action in raising expectations for achievement. The first two focus on the student body as a whole, as raising standards for the entire school comes before raising standards for individuals and subgroups.

Examine Current Rigor Within the School

In order to gauge the level of rigor in your school, begin by planning a work session where grade-level teams or content teams study the results of standardized assessments to include SAT, AP, state, and district assessments. How are students performing on these tests in comparison to how they are doing in their classes? Then, help team leaders facilitate teams as they examine student work, including class work, projects, quizzes, and tests. Does the level of rigor match or exceed written curriculum standards and objectives? If not, what changes in planning for instruction need to occur? After the work session, set up a time to meet with each team individually to agree upon a plan for change. Make sure all teams in the school are aware of one another's plans for change and set aside some time in SIT meetings to discuss implementation of the plans.

Examine and Standardize Grading Practices

Starting with your leadership team, begin to analyze the variables that are factored into a student's report card grades. Using teachers' grade books, identify and list factors that are outside of the student mastering the written curriculum's learning outcomes. Have team leaders describe the grading practices of their teams and how they envision those changing in order to truly communicate student achievement.

Be sure to address the complications that arise when students are taught either below or above grade level. In most cases, they will be graded against the grade level's standards in which they are instructed instead of the grade level to which they belong. If this is the case, it is crucial that this is clearly communicated to parents. Parents should not read the report card and believe that their child has earned a B on grade-level curriculum when, in fact, it is based on below level content. Further, school leaders should question a situation in which a student working below grade level, for years at a time, consistently earns As and Bs. I would argue that it is time to increase the level of challenge, moving the child closer to grade level, even if it means lowered grades. The priority needs to be getting students working on or above grade level, not giving students high grades.

Together with team leaders, plan a staff work session to present the current state of grading in the school versus the ideal state. Then plan to provide teams with time to discuss and agree upon needed changes as well as share those with the rest of the staff. Subsequent sessions should be planned to address problems and questions that arise during implementation.

Create an Effective Instructional Support Team

Most schools have some type of pre-referral process that aims to help classroom teachers better meet the needs of struggling students, while keeping superfluous special education testing to a minimum. An effective team can become a powerful inspiration for what is possible in student achievement when we teach effectively. The intention is worthwhile. But it is the execution that oftentimes fails to fulfill the intention. While the specifics of the process may differ from school to school, there are common characteristics and common mistakes in the implementation across schools. Most schools include the following steps in some form:

- ◆ Problem identification
- ◆ Problem prioritization
- ◆ Goal setting
- ◆ Intervention planning
- ◆ Intervention execution
- ◆ Student growth assessment
- ◆ Intervention adjustment
- ◆ Student release or referral for testing

These steps mirror the Plan, Do, Study, Act cycle that is imperative for schools to utilize in order to continuously improve. But as with any idea, the execution either makes or breaks its success. The following implementation mistakes can make any school's Instructional Support Team powerless to impact what's happening in classrooms. Avoiding them will ensure that your team is valued by and, therefore, used by teachers.

- ◆ **Undervaluing the role and potential impact of the team.** A school without an Instructional Support Team is like a hospital without an emergency room. It has no place for immediate academic crises that demand immediate action. Through an effective IST, lives can literally be saved by getting students out of dire learning situations and putting them back on track academically. Unfortunately, some teachers view the IST as just another school committee that requires attendance. School leaders can show teachers the worth of the team by being personally invested, attending and actively participating in the meetings.

- ◆ **Forcing the team to meet on its own time.** If the team is of significant value to the school, act like it by providing time for them to meet during the school day. As a principal, I began the weekly meeting 45 minutes before teachers' contractual day ended by having instructional assistants cover team members' classrooms or having team members distribute their students to other classrooms. Anyone was, of course, free to leave after 45 minutes, even if the meeting was still going, but most of the time, all members stayed until the meeting came to a natural close. Giving the team 45 minutes to meet, even though it often wasn't enough time, increased members' willingness to work hard, get results, and devote extra time.

- ◆ **Putting the wrong people on the team.** This isn't the time to ask for a volunteer from each team in the school and then hope for the best. Selection for the IST must be strategic, and come with a personal invitation from the principal. The team should consist of all special educators, reading specialists, school psychologists, speech and language pathologists, guidance counselors, two or three expert classroom teachers, one assistant principal, and the principal. You will need your most skilled professionals to support the teachers who utilize the team. After all, their charge will be to analyze classroom situations in which students aren't succeeding and then create practical and effective solutions that regular educators can implement.

- ◆ **Expecting teachers to utilize the team without feeling accountable for achievement.** A culture of accountability must be developed before teachers can be expected to use the IST. After all, the aim of the team is to provide a collaborative environment in which teachers can receive help with teaching students who are struggling academically. If teachers don't believe it is their responsibility to ensure high levels of learning, what incentive would they have for giving their time and energy to the process? If teachers know your expectation (that all students meet or exceed grade-level standards) and they know that student achievement will be scrutinized carefully during the year through pacing conferences, teachers will willingly seek support in order to succeed.

♦ **Spending too much time in problem identification.** While it's true that if you don't correctly identify the problem, the rest of the process is futile, there should be limits to the time spent in this phase. Nothing turns a teacher off more than having to bring her case back to the team week after week and getting nowhere. The only reason for putting off problem identification is if the team requires more specific information or data about the student that the teacher hasn't brought to the meeting.

♦ **Creating complicated interventions and assessments.** Teachers need help in focusing their efforts in smart and efficient ways. They will not utilize a team that expects them to implement complex interventions and administer assessments that are time consuming to make, administer, and assess. The team must be creative in finding simple, easy to implement solutions.

♦ **Allowing goals that are not academic in nature.** Although some students discussed in IST may have secondary behavior issues, this team is not the place for problem-solving that focuses upon behavior problems or parent problems. It is a place for solving academic problems, which requires it to develop academic goals. For instance, the student will increase her sight word vocabulary from 13 words to 40 words in four weeks. Students who have behavior issues as a primary concern should be referred to the school's Student Services Team instead, where appropriate goals and plans that address conduct can be developed.

♦ **Failing to follow up.** Most academic goals that are developed span approximately four to six weeks, after which the teacher comes back to the team to share whether or not the goal was met. At that point, another goal can be developed, or if the student is already back on track, the case can be dismissed. Following up on each case is crucial to keeping track of student progress toward the goals that are set. The follow-up date should be set as soon as the goal is written. Failure to follow up eliminates accountability for the teacher and the IST.

It is also critical to conduct walk-throughs of classrooms to observe the agreed-upon interventions as they are implemented. One time a teacher came to her follow-up meeting and admitted that she hadn't implemented the agreed-upon intervention at all. She just hadn't been sure of when to do it and

Opportunity for Reflection

How standardized are the grading practices in your school? Are there teachers you would identify as easy graders or tough graders? What can you do in the weeks ahead to begin to address these differences?

Reflect on the state of special education in your school. What can be done to develop shared accountability for identified students' progress between special and regular educators? What can you do to increase the expertise of both special and regular educators?

Reflect upon your own Instructional Support Team. Is it being utilized by teachers? Is it getting results that are increasing teacher efficacy? What can you do to make it a more effective team?

what to do with the rest of the class. If I had visited her room regularly during that four weeks, I would have probably noticed that the intervention wasn't happening. At the very least though, I would have casually asked her about it, giving her the opportunity to discuss the roadblocks she faced. Providing follow-up gives teachers the support and guidance needed to follow through with actions to which they've committed.

8

Fearless Decision: Prioritizing Results Over Ideology

The Encarta World English Dictionary (2009) defines ideology as a "meaningful belief system: a set of beliefs, values, and opinions that shapes the way a person or a group such as a social class thinks, acts, and understands the world." It sounds like a positive thing, and it can be. Adopting particular ideologies helps us define ourselves and the world around us, providing a distinct point-of-view. It simplifies complex issues and gives us a sense of belonging and meaning. But blind allegiance to any ideology can be dangerous, focusing people on emotional rhetoric rather than on productive action. The dark side of ideology drives hatred, terrorism, and violence around the globe. And in the U.S., warring political ideologies have divided people unlike any other time in recent history. The opposing sides cannot seem to soften their beliefs enough to compromise for the good of the country. In fact, it is just this reality that Senator Evan Bayh of Indiana commented on when resigning, stating of Washington D.C. politics, "There is too much partisanship and not enough progress—too much narrow ideology and not enough practical problem-solving" (Cillizza, 2010). Regardless of personal political beliefs, I think people on both sides of the aisle would agree with the sentiment of Bayh's remark. The country expects more of its leaders. They have to do better.

Rival Ideologies

Unfortunately, a similar climate has hijacked the field of education, causing professionals in each core content area to clash over what should be taught, as well as how it should be taught. While disagreements over pedagogy have existed for a long time—certainly since Dewey challenged traditional thinking with his progressive ideas—the current ideological divide, still rooted in this divergence, has taken discord to a new level. Open rancor has seized many schools, demanding that teachers take sides and defend one particular way of teaching. The dreary results of the Trends in International Mathematics and Science Study (TIMSS) in the early 1990s stoked the fire within the mathematics world. On one side of the argument were traditionalists who put emphasis on practicing math facts and skills, as well as memorizing algorithms. Linda Starr (2002) describes the opposing views in her article "Math Wars": "On the other side [were] proponents of what is often called 'whole math,' who deride the old 'kill and drill' methods of education, claiming that children learn best when they discover, understand, and integrate knowledge through independent exploration." This same debate has resurged time and time again.

In her book *The Academic Achievement Challenge*, Jeanne Chall (2000) describes the seemingly never-ending debate over reading instruction, starting in the early 1900s, between those who believe in early skill instruction versus those who believe that instruction in basic skills makes students dislike reading: "They abhorred rote learning. Concern with the phonological aspects of reading was seen then—as it is now, unfortunately—by whole-language proponents as pulling the reader away from understanding and toward rote learning. Therefore, it was to be avoided" (p. 66). The disagreements got more heated with President George W. Bush's Reading First legislation, which required districts to adopt scientifically-proven instructional practices for reading. And still today, the reading and math wars play themselves out daily in classrooms from kindergarten to college, leaving many teachers caught uncomfortably in the middle.

When one educator was an undergraduate, he was taught one particular reading methodology by his reading professors. There was no room for questioning or consideration of other methodologies. Then, in his senior year, he began his student teaching assignment where he was paired with a mentor who had gone through the same college program as he. One of the first things his mentor whispered to him was, "Please don't tell the professors how I'm teaching reading. They would never forgive me."

In response, he asked, "Is your way working?"

With a grin, she answered, "Yes!"

Groupthink

One urban administrator saw first-hand the damage that can come from ideological wars: the snuffing out of common sense with narrow cultural norms, the sanctioned behavioral patterns. Upon being assigned to the secondary school, she had examined the incoming assessment data and was alarmed at the number of students unable to pass course assessments. Investigating the situation further, she found that in years prior the faculty had been focused on learning and utilizing a particular brand of student questioning strategies. Time had been put into workshops, along with follow-up activities, and the faculty was dedicated to making them work to the exclusion of some basics. So when this principal began to ask teachers how they were intervening to address the poor achievement in course content, the responses told a story of the cultural norms that had been developed.

- ◆ "We're using more of the new questioning techniques. Right now, it's more important that students like being in class."
- ◆ "We stopped going by the curriculum a while ago. We try to let the students determine what's important to learn, and we support them with our questioning strategies."
- ◆ "We're not allowed to use much direct instruction. It has to be all constructivist."

After more digging, she discovered that the original intention of the professional development had been to offer students more opportunities for higher-level thinking and give them the chance to relate learning to personal interests. There had never been an intention to develop practices that would supersede teaching the written curriculum. But over time, this is exactly what occurred. Teachers afraid of getting into trouble for using practices they thought were frowned upon adopted teaching practices that they perceived would be acceptable to their supervisors and their peers.

Requiring strict adherence to a particular ideology or withdrawing approval from those who deviate can create anxiety among teachers and rob them of the freedom to choose instructional practices that will benefit their particular students. If, as school leaders, we truly believe that students learn differently, then how could we hold up one way of teaching as the only acceptable way?

Another long-term consequence of strictly adhering to one ideology is a school of teachers—or a district of teachers and leaders—who blindly defend it at all costs, the highest of those costs being student learning. As in the previous example, a limited paradigm can become the basis of powerful cultural norms that stunt valuable ideas and take priority over actual improvement. It is just this reality that Irving Janis, a forefather in the study of group dynamics, labeled "groupthink" in his 1970s research. Janis described eight symptoms of groupthink that, unfortunately, many will recognize in their own schools and organizations today:

1. Illusion of Invulnerability: Members ignore obvious danger, take extreme risk, and are overly optimistic.
2. Collective Rationalization: Members discredit and explain away warning contrary to group thinking.
3. Illusion of Morality: Members believe their decisions are morally correct, ignoring the ethical consequences of their decisions.
4. Excessive Stereotyping: The group constructs negative stereotypes of rivals outside the group.
5. Pressure for Conformity: Members pressure any in the group who express arguments against the group's stereotypes, illusions, or commitments, viewing such opposition as disloyalty.
6. Self-Censorship: Members withhold their dissenting views and counter-arguments.
7. Illusion of Unanimity: Members perceive falsely that everyone agrees with the group's decision; silence is seen as consent.
8. Mindguards: Some members appoint themselves to the role of protecting the group from adverse information that might threaten group complacency. (Janis & Mann, 1979)

Groupthink may develop over time in school districts and schools where certain cultural norms are in place. Organizational coach and strategist Sherry Schiller (2008) states that all stakeholders, including teachers and administrators figure out "how people are really expected to behave" and "quickly learn the unspoken 'rules of engagement.' When they move from one school to another, they re-learn which expectations and behaviors to bring with them, which to leave, and which to develop."

E.D. Hirsch (1996) views the groupthink situations found in schools as having national roots, the results of a larger intellectual monopoly:

Our American experience demonstrates that an intellectual monopoly which requires conformity of ideas is more stultifying than a merely institutional one. Despite the myth of local control, the intellectual monopoly ruling American K–12 education is more pervasive and harmful than the merely bureaucratic control exercised in other liberal democracies. Its prevailing ideas are more extreme and

Opportunity for Reflection

Reflect upon your school. Are there any ideological battles being waged between or among departments or grades?

Have dominant ideologies created any kind of groupthink in your school? How open is your faculty to different teaching methodologies?

process-dominated than those found in systems that are more successful than our own. (p. 65)

Jeanne Chall (2000) also notes the widespread and continued support of ideologies in the education community at large that have not panned out as superior when compared to other methodologies. For example, "although the NAEP findings indicate that our children have grave deficiencies in the most basic aspects of school subjects, the current focus is away from teaching these and toward teaching broader concepts" (p. 67). Moreover, she points out a dysfunctional pattern in education leaders of ignoring information that could impact classroom practices.

Why, then, do we end up researching the same questions . . . time and time again? Why, one might reasonably ask, do we not accept the research findings and base our instruction on it? For an answer to this question we must consider the other powerful forces (besides reason and common sense) that influence practice, namely, values, ideologies, philosophies, and appealing rhetoric. (p. 65–66)

Why do we prioritize ideology over results?

Need for Acceptance vs. Fear of Rejection

Many school leaders unknowingly began to adopt ideologies in college, while learning the field from professors who taught their content from a singular perspective, rather than from multiple viewpoints. This way of thinking may have been extended into a first teaching experience by aligning with that of the new school. Most young educators wouldn't even be aware of any competing ideologies. But even if they were, choosing allegiance to the dominant ideology of one's field and workplace produces feelings of belonging and acceptance. To be a trusted member of the team and to move ahead professionally, many feel the pressure to conform.

The same pressure exists for experienced leaders. If principals were to try a methodology outside of the dominant thinking, they could easily face the rejection of both teachers and colleagues. For many administrators who may already work in a stressful and conflict-rich environment, the fear of being rejected by colleagues is too painful to bear.

Need for a Sense of Meaning and Purpose vs. Fear of Purposelessness

When leaders remain focused on teaching rather than on learning, then ideology takes on great importance. Leaders can view their job as supporting and furthering the correct doctrine of practice. Directing teachers in the "how" of teaching is what many school administrators think they are hired to do—and in part, it's true. Asking principals to refrain from telling teachers how to teach would cause immediate feelings of purposelessness. In fact, focusing on classroom practice is what leads school leaders to spend much of their time planning professional development for their teachers and then using precious time with their faculties to provide it. While professional development is an essential part of any profession—helping workers to improve their performance—professional development in the field of education can require large portions of time, yet fail to deliver large gains in student achievement. Although leaders' execution of professional development has improved and much of it is now job-embedded and ongoing, it still hasn't produced significant results. Why?

It Is a Rehash of Dominant Ideologies

Much of the professional development I experienced as a teacher fell short of introducing concepts and understandings that were authentically unique and/or based on objective research findings. Instead, much of the content is a new version of broad information that just about all educators have heard before, perhaps presented in a more up-to-date wrapping. Leaders may continue to provide this kind of learning opportunity because they haven't seen staff implement chosen practices. However, there are a plethora of reasons to explain why teachers fail to change daily actions. The solution is not to repeat the same information, louder and longer.

It Focuses on the Why (Ideology) vs. the How

In order to change teacher action, which can improve student learning, professional development should focus on training teachers how to do things differently in their classrooms—how to implement effective strategies. Instead, professional development often focuses on the *what* and the *why* (Cole, 2004, p. 3). This only serves to add more ideology and dogma to the school culture, when practical solutions are needed.

It Is Not Based on Objective Need Analysis

Every school's data (both from teacher evaluations and from student assessment) tells a story—a story of what teachers are doing well, along with what they could improve upon. Often, it points to simple areas of everyday practice that could be easily addressed, like adhering to curriculum standards and objectives or using daily classroom data and information to plan for the next day's instruction. But this compelling information is largely ignored by some school leaders when planning professional development, along with teachers who request professional development in favor of selecting broad topics that are "hot" in the industry. So instead of taking common sense steps to reflect and improve practice, schools chase after each new educational idea as if it will be the silver bullet that will fix everything. We've all seen the study group that's based upon the latest professional book, which may or may not hold the solutions to the school's instructional issues or to individual teacher's performance needs. Still, much time is spent having teachers read and discuss the pedagogical content. Further, there is little time for teachers to actually figure out how they might implement the practice or methodology before the focus changes once again. Professional development efforts become more of a distraction than an aid. In an *Education Week* article, Mike Schmoker (2010) commented on this penchant to latch onto the latest pedagogical craze while abandoning common sense methods that would dramatically increase learning: "For decades, we have put novelty and the false god of innovation above our most obvious, proven priorities." He specifically pointed out that "the consistent delivery of lessons that include multiple checks for understanding may be the most powerful, cost-effective action we can take to ensure learning." The power of improving simple professional practices based on what is observed during day-to-day walk-throughs, as well as in student data, cannot be overlooked.

It Doesn't Require or Monitor Action

"If one accepts that to 'develop' one must at some point show evidence of learning by doing something differently, then most formal professional development does not develop anyone. At best, it leads to an awareness that change is needed" (Cole, 2004, p. 3). As in the study group example, many professional development opportunities include presenting information and discussing information. Few go further. The outcome of effective P.D. should include specific implementation actions within a specified time frame. These

> ### *Opportunity for Reflection*
>
> How has the fear of purposelessness or rejection influenced decisions you've made regarding your school's instructional practices?

focus practices should be observable with classroom walk-throughs, and their effectiveness should be monitored by the grade-level team.

It Uses the Time that Could Be Spent in the Plan, Do, Study, Act Cycle

One shared problem in the field of education is limited time. This situation requires school leaders to be strategic about how available time is utilized. When discussing the importance of selecting instructional practices, implementing them, and then monitoring their impact on student achievement, many exasperated administrators say, "When do we fit that in?" The answer is that it can't be fit in amongst everything else that competes for time. Instead, this process must take priority and replace other processes occurring in the school.

When one shifts from trying to control all instructional practices to a focus on results, then the *how* is allowed to vary from teacher to teacher, school to school. And leaders are free to spend their time exploring the research on various methodologies and leading strategic and tactical conversations about improving achievement through focused action. So how do we move past limiting ideologies to focus on results?

Antidote: Develop the Courage to Prioritize Results Over Ideology

Set Your Intention

The first step in setting a new intention to prioritize results is to recognize the unconscious ideologies that provide the foundation for your educational point-of-view. These professional preferences are not bad. Indeed, they help to form the bedrock of your professional values. But they must be fully acknowledged and disclosed in order to monitor their control over your thinking. Consider the philosophies of college professors, principals, and other leaders that have influenced and shaped you as a developing educator.

Also reflect upon the philosophies you see being played out in your school, district, and on the national scene. Here are a few to consider:

- Student-centered vs. teacher-centered
- Traditional vs. progressive/constructivist
- Knowledge or content-rich vs. thinking process-oriented

What are the strengths and weaknesses of each orientation? And what are the risks to students of an allegiance to a singular ideology? This focus on what's best for students will transform lower concerns of supporting and pleasing powerful interests within the field to higher concerns in which you are not the center. Adopting a "whatever it takes" attitude in helping students will require an open mind and a willingness to select appropriate strategies—no matter what ideology they are rooted in. This freeing new orientation and the increased learning that accompanies it will produce the self-worth that all school leaders, and all people for that matter, seek. But you can't go it alone.

Find a Mentor

Breaking a groupthink atmosphere takes both mental and emotional fortitude. Before you can begin overcoming it in your school, you must have a support system for yourself. My mentors were colleagues both inside and outside the district. And without their ongoing help, I would have been able to accomplish very little. One of the strengths of groupthink is its ability to make the group's thought seem right and opposing thought seem wrong. This can leave you questioning yourself, even when your personal convictions run deep. In these moments, your mentor will be able to listen to you with an open mind and provide you with an outside opinion—a reality check. These reality checks can do wonders to boost your confidence during tough times and give you constructive criticism when needed, building professional judgment over time. In order to see mentors in action, visit their schools and watch them first hand. Conducting informal walk-throughs with them is a powerful way to see teaching and learning through their lens.

When choosing a mentor, the following character traits should be sought out:

- **Independent-thinking:** In order to support you in recognizing and overcoming accepted ideological views, your mentor should be a strong and independent thinker—someone who has already broken through negative cultural norms in his or her professional life. He or she should be refreshed by new ideas that diverge from common thought.

◆ **Results-driven:** Mentors should be leaders who have proven track records of high academic achievement in their schools. They must value the information provided by standardized testing and other forms of assessment as gauges of teacher effectiveness, rather than negating the value of such information. They must teach staff to value all data, appreciating the insights it provides while acknowledging its limitations.

◆ **Courageous:** It may seem a bit overdramatic to some to list courage as a necessary trait for a mentor in the field of education. It isn't as if we are soldiers going off to war in a foreign country or police officers apprehending an armed suspect. However, instead of risking one's life, the education leader who acts in alignment with personal convictions risks keeping positive relationships with teachers and colleagues. In order to move people beyond negative or limiting cultural norms, one must be willing to take this risk. Mentors' decisions should be based on what they feel is best for students, instead of ideas that happen to be popular within the field or district. Because they will make decisions that are sometimes unpopular, these leaders must be willing to take criticism both from colleagues and school staff. They must prioritize helping students above emotional comfort or personal gain.

◆ **Willing to invest in others:** In order for others to benefit from mentors' knowledge and skill, they must be willing to share it with others. These leaders must be motivated by helping to create success in others. This can be seen in the time spent developing the capacity of teachers and leaders within the school. While some mentor relationships develop naturally over time without any labels of mentor and mentee, some professional relationships are more formal. Ask the leader you have in mind if he or she would consider becoming a mentor to you. In formalizing the relationship, opportunities to meet can be scheduled and plans can be made to study particular issues. Keep in mind that some mentor relationships are short-term, while others are long-term, depending on need, availability, and the situation at hand.

After setting your own intention and finding a source of professional support, it's time to build trust with faculty and staff.

Build Trust

When building trust, keep in mind that although you've committed to having an open mind, your faculty hasn't yet. It will be necessary to lay the groundwork for flexible thinking by exhibiting an attitude of non-judgment toward the instructional practices within the building. When one teacher complains about another's teaching methods, respond by reminding him that methods are expected to vary and that the results of that instruction—not the instruction itself—is what will be examined. No one will be considered a bad teacher for trying a new method or experimenting with a more traditional one.

Campaign: Identify the Pain and the Gain

To identify the current pain that teachers feel, examine the way faculty and staff treat each other and explore the relationship between faculty and the administration. Do teachers within and across teams support and trust one another? Have they had a history of trust with administrators? In many cases, you will find staff members who have not been encouraged to think divergently about their practices. Instead, it's likely they've been told what to do and how to do it. Even worse, the favored strategies have most likely changed each year, leaving teachers frustrated and exhausted. This is teachers' **pain**. If curriculum is aligned with assessments and teachers teach the curriculum, then how they deliver it should be up to them. This is their **gain**. First in leadership teams and then in pacing conferences, examine data together to determine areas of needed change in instruction. Then, collaboratively review the research together and choose new instructional methods to create breakthrough achievement.

Show Clear Contrast

Prioritizing ideology over results is a decision that impacts and stigmatizes students. Schools that stick to a narrow ideology are averse to substantive change, which is the only kind of change that will make a difference in achievement. Those who adhere to the same ways of doing things believe there must be something inherently wrong with the student who isn't learning. Schools that prioritize results over rhetoric believe that all students learn differently and that it is the job of the teaching team to find methodologies that work.

Build Expertise Together

Although you will have spent the time to build trust, identify teachers' pain/ gain, and show clear contrast, there may still be some hold-outs who are comfortable with engrained ideologies, the way things have been for a long time. These teachers will need clear evidence to be convinced that drawing from various philosophies increases learning. This will come in time through reviewing rigorous research and participating in a Plan, Do, Study, Act cycle. For dealing with this problem, I prefer Tim Connors' (2004) "See It, Own It, Solve It, Do It" cycle, introduced in Chapter 6, for its powerful focus on accountability.

In the "See It" stage, the available data is analyzed. The next stage, "Own It"—the most important for opening minds—is where the team comes to terms with the fact that low areas of performance are due to the team's instruction. In owning those low scores, teachers understand that some of their chosen methodologies may not be the most effective, at least for their current students. In the "Solve It" stage, new practices are devised in an ideology-free zone and then implemented in the "Do It" stage. I suggest that this simple process be the basis for most conversations, meetings, and professional development during the school year.

We Have All We Need

Most of us already have all we need to turn achievement around in our schools. This is more than a fuzzy, positive affirmation. It is the hard truth. We have the time and we have the expertise. Competent teachers currently own enough of the professional knowledge they need to improve learning in their classrooms. While there are times when it is necessary to learn from sources outside the school, in general, teachers don't need to hear speakers, go to conferences, or participate in other programmatic professional development to begin increasing student learning now. So why don't they? Because what they do need is the time to collaborate with peers, resource teachers and administrators in their own buildings, to critically examine their practices. Much of the time, teachers need to participate in this reflective process—it's just used for other priorities.

So begin by restructuring the way time is utilized within the building, narrowing the focus to achievement. This reflective process should be done with your leadership team, since they will participate in SIT meetings and faculty meetings and will be responsible for facilitating the time carved out for team meetings. I suggest the following uses for traditional meeting times:

School Improvement Team Meetings

As stated previously, monthly SIT meetings should be used to help increase student achievement—period. Other issues should be brought forward at separate Team Leaders meetings, designed for the purpose of dealing with non-achievement topics. At the end of the year, collaboratively analyze all incoming data and allow team leaders to create simple one page plans for new teacher actions to address the areas of need. During the school year, use the "See It, Own It, Solve It, Do It" cycle to analyze new data and make changes to the SIT plan. Yes, actually change the written plan. Have your team leaders cross through strategic actions that aren't working, discuss those with the leadership team, and replace the actions with new ones. Work to solve any problems that arise with implementation of these new strategies.

Faculty Meetings

Abandon canned professional development presentations in favor of authentic development that will lead to teacher action and student learning. Monthly after-school or before-school time can be used to:

- Allow grade-level teams time to discuss problems and successes in the implementation of strategic actions in the SIT plan. (How does it look in your classroom? How often are you doing it? How can I make it work in my room?)
- Allow grade-level teams to conduct lesson studies in order to plan together and improve the implementation of specified practices.
- Allow grade-level teams to analyze student work together. These artifacts will show, before any formal assessments are given, whether or not student learning has improved—and if standards are consistently high among team members.
- Allow vertical teaming between grade levels.
- Allow teams to walk through classrooms together, analyzing posted student work for evidence of particular learning or for level of rigor.
- Allow teams to better familiarize themselves with their own curriculum, as well as that of the grade or course before and after their own.
- Present new and needed information to the faculty regarding how to implement practices of interest (based on objective need).

Team Meetings

Team meetings are often used by teachers to discuss administrative issues like schedule changes, planning the details of field trips, ordering and organizing materials, etc. If time is left after those issues are squared away, then teachers may use the time to plan together. Usually, this planning consists of teachers sharing resources for an upcoming unit or topic. But that's as far as it gets. In order to use team meeting time for activities that increase achievement, different tactics must be utilized by team leaders.

- Take care of administrative issues via email, lunchroom conversation, notes, etc. instead of during team meeting time.

◆ Instead of planning in a generalized fashion, respond to student learning as a team. Share the results of formal and informal assessments and plan instruction to meet the specific learning needs that arise. Agree on how and when the new instructional practices will take place. Then, afterwards, examine student work once again to evaluate the effectiveness of the instruction.

A simple agenda for team meetings could be:

1. What is our current data telling us?
2. How will we respond? What will we do instructionally?
3. How will we know if it worked?

Mike Schmoker (2000) describes a similar team meeting format: "The general purpose proposed for these meetings is to identify major concerns and strategies to promote better results for an agreed upon goal" (p. 119). He suggests discussing "strategies that worked, chief challenges, and proposed solutions" (p. 120). Finally, Schmoker recommends developing an action plan for what each teacher will do before the next meeting. Although team leaders can't directly control what goes on in team members' classrooms, when meetings consist of these actions and discussions, instruction in all classrooms will change. When team members know they will be asked to share the results of implemented strategies, along with student work samples, they will almost always try the strategies. Meetings such as these increase accountability by influencing the daily practice of teachers.

Substitute Time

Most school leaders have access to funds in order to pay for substitute teachers throughout the school year. Get the biggest bang for your buck by providing paid time for each team to meet for a half day after any benchmark or formative assessments have been given. If it's the first time using a particular assessment, give teams time to score them together using a concise rubric. In this way, teachers will grade student work consistently. Once teachers are familiar with the required assessments, then they should arrive at the half-day sessions with their class assessments pre-graded. The time can then be used to determine team strengths and weaknesses by finding trends in the test data. From there, just as in every other meeting, teachers can then determine how they will address low areas of achievement. Other uses for substitute time include peer coaching for the implementation of specific teaching methods and having teams conduct walk-throughs of the building for specific learning purposes.

Opportunity for Reflection

What are some ways to show teachers that you are open-minded to various instructional methodologies? How might that influence the culture of your school?

Reflect upon how time is currently used throughout your school. Are there activities that can be replaced with a "See It, Own It, Solve It, Do It" cycle?

Keeping and sharing an open mind about pedagogy, including both traditional and progressive practices, will alleviate teacher fears associated with risk-taking in the work environment. When results are the one and only determination of a practice's worth rather than personal preference or industry hype, then teacher capacity will be elevated along with self-worth.

Conclusion

On January 2, 2011, the country lost one of its fearless leaders, Major Dick Winters. Winters, the subject of much of Stephen Ambrose's work, led Easy Company through some of the toughest battles of World War II's European theatre. In the middle of life-threatening chaos, his unassuming courage inspired the confidence and loyalty of the men of the 101st Airborne Division. He set the highest expectations for his company's performance, held them accountable to achieve the goals of each operation, addressed conflict as it arose, and took decisive action. Awarded the Distinguished Service Cross, he played an essential role in defeating Hitler and bringing peace to Europe and the United States, preserving our freedom and way of life.

Although professional educators in our schools aren't soldiers on the battlefield, they do seek the same authentic leadership that can that can inspire and guide them through tough circumstances and increasing pressures. There is much at stake in public education and little time to fix it. Gone are the days of teachers who just want principals to make their professional lives easy. Today's modern educators desire more for themselves and demand more from school leaders. Teachers' success relies upon their ability to improve the lives and futures of the students they serve, and they expect effective leadership to guide them to that end. They want their chosen vocation, their career, to be of value—because then they claim a sense of worth.

It is, indeed, a brave leader who can overcome his own buried fears, as well as those of his faculty, in order to experience the internal reward of true success as a school administrator. During the writing of this book, I've come across many educators who are doing just that—setting new intentions and expectations, acknowledging fears as they arise, and enduring the discomfort of fear long enough to see inklings of positive change emerge. They act as models for courageous action, inspiring fearlessness in their teachers. My hope is that this trend continues across the country, creating schools that are worth our children attending, those that can truly prepare students for the challenges facing them in the world of work and post-secondary education.